Sacred Ring
Pagan Origins of British Folk Festivals & Customs

By Michael Howard

Sacred Ring
Pagan Origins of British Folk Festivals & Customs

©1995 Michael Howard

ISBN 1 898307 28 8

Also by Michael Howard, Published by Capall Bann:
Angels & Goddesses
Mysteries of the Runes
The Pickingill papers

Cover design by Daryth Bastin
Cover illustration by Nigel Jackson

Published by:

Capall Bann Publishing
Freshfields
Chieveley
Berks
RG16 8TF

Contents

Chapter One

From Paganism to Christ

In the West today we live in a technologically advanced, materialistic consumer society in which, in Britain, only about ten per cent of the population follow an established religion. The rest are either following alternative forms of spirituality, are agnostics or atheists or are nominal 'Christians' who pay lip service to the moral values of the Church at christenings, marriages and funerals. In such a desacralised society, where the majority of people live in cities and towns, most of the population is cut off from the countryside and from the source of food production which was an integral focus of our ancestor's lives.

Before the Industrial Revolution, and the mass exodus from the countryside that followed it as the new factories were built, most people belonged to what a Marxist would term 'the peasant class' and earned their living from the land and its bounty. In rural areas children were brought up on farms knowing all about 'the facts of life' from an early age and they had no illusions about where their daily bread came from. Today some inner city children think milk is made in a factory and have no concept of the process that transforms an animal grazing in a field into a shrink-wrapped steak in a supermarket.

I remember reading a few years ago of a scheme to bring city children on 'adventure holidays' based in the countryside. The organisers encountered problems because many of the children were scared of the dark, frightened of climbing hills or just plain terrified by the silence and the open spaces. Such psychotic reactions are a terrible indictment of a society cut off from its natural roots, where residents on new housing estates ask the builders not to plant trees because 'it is so messy to clear up the leaves'.

The contrast with the lives of our grandparents and great grandparents even a hundred years ago cannot be more striking. Those who lived in the country were aware of the changing patterns of the seasons and the natural cycle of the agricultural year. As we shall see in this book, they actively celebrated this cycle in folk rituals that had been handed down for generations. These rituals marked the turning of the Wheel of the Year, from Yule at midwinter, through to the spring equinox, midsummer, early autumn with its harvest celebrations, to the beginning of winter and the dark season.

When we talk of 'folk ritual' and 'folklore' what exactly do we mean? The dictionary definition of folklore gives us 'the traditional beliefs of the people', while 'folk ritual' could be defined, using the same criteria, as 'the religious practices of the people'. Even a cursory glance at the seasonal customs described in this book shows that the type of religion involved was not the Christian one, although often Christian symbolism and practice has been overlaid on them. Behind the rather transparent attempts to justify some folk rites as the commemoration of historical events or local incidents within recent memory, exists a deep and darker tradition, one rooted in pre-Christian beliefs and the ancient worship of the land, its elemental spirits and Gods.

Attempts have been made by historians, and some folklorists, to prove that this or that folk ritual or seasonal custom is of recent origin and is therefore not truly representative of older beliefs and practices. They point out that folk traditions such as the May Day revels, with the Green Man or the Jack-in-the-Hedge, were at their heyday in the late 18th and early 19th centuries. Likewise many popular Christmas customs, with alleged pagan origins and overtones, were a result of the Victorians, influenced by their creation of childhood and the novels and short stories of Charles Dickens.

This is, of course, a fact of folk history, but it is one that can be interpreted in several different ways. It is fact that there was a spirited revival of folk traditions in the 19th century. This was led by such pioneers as Cecil Sharp, who founded the English Folk Song & Dance Society and revived the dying art of Morris dancing, and artistic intellectuals like John Ruskin. It was Ruskin who imported from southern Europe the well-known Maypole dance with children weaving ribbons around it. However, and this is an important point, neither Sharp nor Ruskin invented May Day and the Maypole or even Morris dancers. They were merely modern revivers of old traditions and customs which had been neglected over the years and in some cases nearly died out.

Another argument put forward by the sceptics is that many of the first references to folk traditions and rites of allegedly pagan origin only date back to the late Middle Ages. A possible reason for this lack of information can be provided by the fact that it was not until the invention of the printing press that knowledge about cultural matters became more widespread. As it was, writing and the written word was in the control of a section of society (the

Church) who would have been less then happy to give free publicity to the survival, and widespread popularity, of rites and beliefs, often of a bawdy and orgiastic nature, which had their genesis in the pagan Old Religion. It is often said that history is written by the conquerors and the Church's treatment of pagan survivals and survivalists can be compared to the distortion of Jewish cultural history by the Nazis.

Historians, with a few notable exceptions, are also keen to suggest to their readers that the new religion was widely accepted within a short time of its arrival in this country. Of course it all depends on when you believe Christianity arrived on our shores. As I have pointed out in my previous book *Angels and Goddesses* (Capall Bann 1994), schoolchildren are taught that St Augustine was sent here at the end of the 6th century by Pope Gregory to convert the English. In fact there is plenty of evidence to suggest that Christianity arrived here in Roman times.

By the time the Roman missionaries arrived to convert the Saxons, Jutes and Angles in southern England the Celtic Church had been established in the western and northern areas of Britain. Celtic Christianity, despite the propaganda of later writers, had not been that successful in converting the pagan tribes and the arrival of the Germanic peoples after the withdrawal of the Roman Eagles had introduced other forms of pagan religion into the country. It was these new pagans, the Celtic pagan survivalists and the Celtic Christian 'heretics' who Augustine and his Roman monks had to combat when his mission landed in Kent in 597 CE.

The early Saxon converts to the new religion often only paid lip service to Christian beliefs. Indeed after the death

4

of Augustine the pagan opposition to the new faith became so strong that the Roman mission had to temporarily flee the country and sought refuge in France. It was only with some reluctance that they returned and even then the Saxon kings and their subjects practised both religions. Where Christianity did appear to triumph the Old Ways were merely driven underground to re-emerge in mutated forms such as witchcraft and folk magic.

In 669 the Pope was forced to send another mission to southern England and this was led by Theodore the Greek, who became the new Archbishop of Canterbury. One of his first actions was to issue a series of laws that forbade pagan practices. One of the most famous of these concerned the wearing of animal masks and costumes during the Twelve Days of Yule and is worth quoting in full.

> *Whoever at the kalends (first) of January goes about in the form of a stag, that is changing himself into the form of an animal, dressing in the skin of a horned beast, and putting on the head of a beast, for those who in such wise transform themselves into the appearance of a wild animal, penance for three years, because it is devilish.*

Unfortunately Theodore's edict did not have a lasting effect for, as we shall see later in this book, in the 1900's men were still going around West Country villages at New Year wearing 'the skin of a horned beast, and putting on the head of a beast.'

Whatever historians tell us, elements of paganism survived in popular culture into the medieval period and beyond. In many cases the continuity of these beliefs was not directly from the past and they existed in the form of folk memories, often misunderstood, misinterpreted and frequently debased. Traditional forms of witchcraft and the folk magic of the village wise women and cunning men often preserved aspects of the Old Ways. However, even these were changed, modified and degraded through the centuries as other influences permeated rural life and its folk culture. The Old Faith was fragmented by the years of persecution and only degenerate remnants survived, often concealed under the guise of seasonal customs and the rural superstitions observed by country folk to mark and record the progress of the agricultural year.

Confusion enters the subject when we come to the modern revival of Wicca which began in the 1800's and probably reached its climax immediately before and after World War II. The major public figure in the present-day revival was Gerald Gardner (d. 1964), a retired Customs officer and rubber planter in the Far East. Without going into too much detail here, it seems certain that Gardner was initiated into a witch coven in the New Forest just before the last war. Gardner subsequently, with the help of others, formulated his own series of seasonal rituals to celebrate the Wheel of the Year which form the focus of what is now modern Wicca.

There is some dispute as to whether or not Gardner and his own coven in the 1950's celebrated the eight sabbats or festivals of the year or just the major Celtic ones of Imbolc (February 1st), Beltane (May 1st), Lughnasadh (August 1st) and Samhain (November 1st). At a recent lecture given by Dr Ronald Hutton at Lampeter university in Wales, he stated as a fact given to him by one of its ex-members that Gardner's coven only celebrated the major sabbats before 1957. Doreen Valiente is on record as saying that in 1952 Gardner asked her to write a Yule ritual for the coven and she duly obliged. He was later to claim in his book *Witchcraft Today* (Rider 1954) that this improvised ritual was of ancient heritage.

Gardner seems to have believed that the solar festivals - the equinoxes and solstices - were a Mediterranean or Middle Eastern import. Others point to the north and the Vikings. It is also often claimed that the Celtic fire festivals are older then the solar ones. In this respect it is very interesting to note that the stone circles erected by the prehistoric megalithic culture, including Stonehenge, are aligned to the equinoxes and the solstices, as well as to the fire festivals and lunar phases.

The festivals that were important to the people we call the Celts, and probably also to pre-Celtic peoples, were those of a nomadic people who drove their cattle to new pasture in the spring, and then brought them back in the late autumn. When the Saxons and later the Vikings came to Britain it seems the general celebration of the solar festivals was revived. This then gives us the present cycle of seasonal festivals in the folk calendar celebrated in both the 'Celtic' and Anglicised areas of the British Isles.

As far as medieval witchcraft is concerned, the evidence provided by the witch trials convinced the Christians that the alleged witches followed - or rather parodied - the feast days of the Church's calendar. In fact the opposite was true, for the witches were following the pattern of the old pagan festivals which had been adopted by the new religion. For instance, one of the Berwick witches in Scotland was accused of 'attending the convention' on Lammas Eve and Hallowe'en, when she danced in the churchyard. This was not that strange when you consider that many of the pre-Reformation churches in Scotland (and elsewhere) were built on druidic sites. This is also why many folk rituals centred on or involved the church and its churchyard.

The Aberdeen witches also met at All Hallows and the Pendle witches met on Samhain (November 1st). In 1662 Isobel Gowdie confessed freely that 'a Grand Meeting was held about the end of each quarter'. There is also some evidence that witches met on the solar festivals as well. In France covens gathered at Easter (the spring equinox) and on St John's Eve, to coincide with midsummer or the summer solstice.

Today many people interested in green issues and the protection of the environment are drawn towards the Craft and neo-paganism. Sadly however they often approach rural matters with a blinkered or rosy-coloured view. Too often when city dwellers and suburbanites relate to Nature and the countryside it is within an artificial framework that encourages and promotes false nostalgia for a 'golden age' of the past and sentimentality for a lifestyle that was often hard, cruel and harsh. Even today the so-called glories of rural life can be so easily blighted by poverty, lack of public transport, rural unemployment and loneliness leading to high suicide rates.

Our ancestors had no illusions about the 'joys of country living'. Out in all weathers, battling against the elements, fighting disease and staving off poverty they knew all about Nature, red in tooth and claw. To them the celebration of the festivals was in some ways an emotional release from hard work, hence the many complaints about the drunkenness, sexual promiscuity and rowdy behaviour often associated with folk customs. It was for this reason that the puritans of the 17th century and the Victorians did their best to repress rural rites.

Where genuine folk customs survive and flourish today it should be noted that they are always performed with serious intent and in the firm belief that either good or bad luck will follow depending on how correctly the rituals were performed. They always involve local people, many of whom have often performed the ritual in their families for generations, and are never staged for tourists, but as an integral part of daily life and the folk culture of the community.

It is a pity that, while claiming ancient pedigrees, the modern pagan movement and Wiccan revival has often failed to link itself with the surviving vestiges of the Old Ways to be found in folklore, seasonal customs and traditional forms of rural witchcraft. The impression exists, rightly or wrongly, of a general lack of understanding about such essential matters as the esoteric symbolism of the Wheel of the Year and its seasonal cycle of festivals.

This is a sad reflection on our materialistic society, where the average person is out of balance with the natural rhythms of the seasons and their annual cycle representing growth, decay and renewal. The acknowledgement and understanding of the Wheel of the Year lies at the heart of any spiritual belief system based on Nature and at the very centre of our existence on this green planet. Properly understood, the Wheel offers a symbolic and literal key to the eternal mysteries of life, death and rebirth. On an inner level it is a blueprint for spiritual development and psychic awareness, ultimately leading to the gnosis of enlightenment.

Old Father Christmas

Chapter Two

Yule to Twelfth Night

Christmas has always been regarded as the most important Christian festival, marking as it does the birthday of Jesus. Until the 4th century CE January 6th was celebrated by the early Christians as the birth date and December 25th was adopted between 336 and 353, to coincide with the celebration of the winter solstice on December 21st. The solstice was the birthday of the young solar god Mithras, whose cultus was a serious threat to early Christianity in the Roman Empire, and it also coincided with the Jewish Festival of Lights on December 20th. The new feast of Christ's Mass was first declared an imperial public holiday in 529 by the Roman Emperor. In 567 the Church announced that the twelve days from December 25th to January 6th, were to be celebrated by all Christians as 'a holy season'.

The many festivities of the Christmas period, extending through into early January, originated in the ancient rituals performed to mark the midwinter solstice. This was the shortest day of the year, or the longest night, when the sun symbolically died and was then reborn from Mother Earth. From this date the days gradually began to lengthen and the sun rose in the sky as the spring equinox approached. Although, paradoxically, the worst of the winter weather in northern climes is still to come, our ancestors knew that the solstice marked an important turning point in the Wheel of the Year. In fact the word 'Yule' is believed to come from the Old Norse 'Jol' and the Old English 'Geol', meaning 'wheel'.

For several centuries prior to the introduction of Mithraism from Persia the Romans had celebrated a festival of winter sowing around the solstice. This ceremony, known as the Saturnalia, was performed, as its name suggests, in honour of Saturn, the god of agriculture and time. It lasted from December 17th to the 24th and during that period all warfare was suspended, businesses closed, executions were postponed and slaves changed places with their masters. It also involved dancing in the streets, heavy drinking, the wearing of animal masks, the parading of phallic images, unbridled sexual licence and the reversal of all social conventions. A faint memory of these orgiastic revels survives today in our Christmas office parties and traditional pantomime, with its gender reversing and cross-dressing.

A Lord of Misrule, usually a slave, was elected to oversee the Saturnalia and he was given complete freedom of action and expression. This ancient custom survived into the post-pagan period. In the reign of the Tudor king Henry VIII a Master of Revels was paid from the royal purse to plan and control the festivities during the Twelve Days of Yule. In this period all rich nobles had their Lords of Misrule, who reigned from Hallowe'en to Candlemas (February 2nd), which is also the dark season of the year ruled by the Old God of the witches in his role as Lord of the Wild Hunt, Holly King and Dark Master of Shadows and Shades.

In the 15th century the Church in France condemned what it called the Festum Fatuorum or Feast of Fools, which it claimed originated in the classical worship of the dual-faced god Janus, the gatekeeper of the Old and New Year. According to the French clergy, priests and clerks even participated wearing masks and dressed as women. They sang 'wanton songs', played dice in church and sat eating black pudding while making 'indecent gestures' during the Mass.

Writing in 1583, Phillip Stubbes, a Puritan who also complained bitterly about the excesses of May Day, described how some local lads elected a 'Captaine of Mischiefe', who in turn selected a bodyguard of young men who wore the 'wanton colour' of green (associated in folk tradition with the Devil, Robin Hood and the faeries). This Lord of Misrule and his retinue then dressed themselves up in lace, scarves and ribbons, tied bells to their feet and with hobby horses, dragons and 'other antiques' danced to the sound of pipes and drums to the local church. To Stubbes disgust the company was joined there by a crowd of merrymakers who danced and feasted in the churchyard until after dark.

The tradition seems to have survived into contemporary times for Sir Walter Scott gives a graphic account of it in his book *The Abbot*, based on his experiences of the custom in Edinburgh. He describes how the Lord of Misrule and his company of knaves, fools and jesters occupied churches, celebrated mock Masses and sang indecent parodies of hymns.

The Lord's court included animal maskers, hobby horses, dancing bears, St George and the Dragon, Robin Hood and his Merry Men, male dancers dressed as women and

Woden Lord of the Wild Hunt

mummers with blackened faces. These folklore characters are also associated with other festivals, such as May Day and Midsummer.

Many of the vestiges of the old Saturnalia were destroyed after the Reformation, when zealous Protestant priests condemned folklore customs as 'Popish heathenism' because they were ironically associated with the Roman Church and its festivals. In the middle of the 17th century the Puritans decreed that Christmas was a heathen festival that should not be celebrated by good Christians. In 1644 they banned all church services on Christmas Day, but when the Roundhead troops tried to forcibly remove Yuletide greenery from houses and close down shops on Christmas Eve people rioted in the streets of London. Although Christmas came back after the restoration of Charles II in 1660, many of its old customs were lost for ever.

December 6th

To Christians this date is the feast of St Nicholas, the patron saint of children, fishermen, sales reps, merchants, bankers, bakers and sailors. Historically, the saint was the Bishop of Myra in Turkey in the 4th century CE and became the national saint of both Greece and Russia. He was a saint who could grant special wishes on his feast day so people lit a candle in his honour and left it burning all night.

The feast day was celebrated by giving small presents and toys to children. It was said that St Nick himself delivered the gifts to those who had been good during the year and this prompted the custom of putting out stockings, or for

The Wild Hunter summons his Hell Hounds

the more optimistic, pillow cases. In Britain, North America and Australia this custom has been transferred to Christmas Eve and it is Santa Claus or Father Christmas who does the honours in the gift giving department.

St Nicholas had been taken across the Atlantic by early Dutch and German settlers and he influenced the popular image of Santa Claus, with his red costume trimmed with white fur, flying sleigh drawn by reindeer etc, which became a favourite illustration in 19th century children's books. This image in turn crossed the Atlantic in Victorian times, when many of the old Christmas customs were revived, and it merged with the late medieval figure of Father Christmas or Father Holly, who featured in the mummer plays. He was a jolly, red-faced fellow with a fat stomach, wearing a red robe, crowned with holly leaves and carrying a knobbly club.

In 1931 Coca-Cola incorporated the new image of Santa Claus into their advertising thus sanitising the figure. Despite this, Santa's traditional costume, his ability to fly, his reindeer and his odd habit of entering and leaving houses by the chimney (in pre-central heating days!) link him with the shamans of northern Europe. In the yurts, or round houses, lived in by the nomadic peoples of Siberia and the Sami of Lapland the smoke hole in the roof is the route used by the spirit of the shaman to enter and leave while he is in trance. White and red, the traditional colours associated with Santa are also the colours of the fly agaric toadstool or sacred mushroom used in shamanic rituals to contact the Otherworld.

Santa also has many characteristics in common with the pagan Lord of Misrule and with the one-eyed god of the runes, Odin or Woden. In Norse mythology Odin is depicted flying through the night skies on his eight-legged steed Sleipnir, bringing gifts to those who have worshipped him during the year. Woden was also the Lord of the Wild Hunt which rides the skies at midwinter collecting the souls of the dead. In early medieval Europe the Wild Hunt was also led by a winter goddess called Frau Holle or Holda. She had command of a company of female spirits

The Vindication of
CHRISTMAS,
OR,
His Twelve Yeares Observations upon the

great and lamentable Tragedy between the King and Parliament; acted by General *Plunder*, and Major General *Tax*;
With his Exhortation to the people; a description of that
oppressing Ringworm called *Excize*; and the manner how
our high and mighty Chriſtmas-Ale that formerly would
knock down *Hercules*, & trip up the heels of a Giant, ſtrook
into a deep Conſumption with a blow from *Weſtminſter*.

Imprinted at London for G. Horton, 1653.

Title page of a 17th century pamphlet supporting
Christmas

called 'the Good Women' who distributed gifts and good luck to the houses they flew over.

December 21st/22nd

This is the date of the winter solstice or Midwinter's Day when the sun enters the Zodiac sign of Capricorn, the Sea Goat. In the Christian calendar it was the feast day of St Thomas, the patron saint of elderly people. It is amusing to note that the Roman god Saturn also ruled old age. On his day people went a-Thomasing, a-gooding or mumping. This was the distribution of small amounts of money to the poor of the parish for them to buy their Christmas fare. Children also went begging for corn, apples and sweets at this time. In Shropshire the Thomas Day gifts were distributed by the members of the parish council or the churchwardens and it was believed those who participated obtained spiritual virtue for the act.

St Thomas' Day was also known as Bellringer's Eve, from the old custom of ringing the church bells to warn people that it was the longest night of the year. As the powers of darkness were supposed to be abroad and at their most potent on this night it was common to spend the evening in company with friends, eating and drinking until the dawn came.

In medieval times it was called 'the night for sharing sins' and God-fearing folk spent it in fasting, prayer and vigil. Knights knelt before the altar of the church, resting their heads on the hilts of their swords and praying for sunrise.

Decorating the Christmas Tree

December 24th

In the old days (e.g. when I was a child in the Fifties!) preparations for Christmas began in earnest on this day and not in early September. It was when the house was garlanded with evergreens and the Christmas Tree was decorated. The practice of hanging up Yuletide greenery comes from the pagan custom of decorating the house at midwinter to symbolise eternal life. The early Church banned the practice but was slowly forced to relent. While holly, yew and laurel have found their way into churches, the humble mistletoe is still banned, except at a special service in York Minster.

The reason is because the plant was sacred to both the Celtic druids and the Teutonic and Norse peoples. Because of its waxy white berries, which resemble drops of semen, it was regarded as a powerful symbol of fertility. The charming custom of 'kissing under the mistletoe bough' is a tame reminder of the erotic symbolism originally associated with it. The druids regarded the plant as a natural healer and for this reason called it the 'All Heal'. Even though the berries are poisonous, modern medical research indicates that they may contain ingredients which have a curative property. In Roman times the historian and naturalist Pliny said that the druids ritually cut down the mistletoe from an oak tree on the sixth night of the new moon with a gold sickle. Sprigs of the plant were laid on the altar at the winter solstice as a gift to the Gods. This may be the origin of the York Minster service where this custom is copied. In Norse mythology the wood of the plant was used to make the arrow used by the trickster fire god Loki to kill the young god of light, Baldur.

The holly and the ivy are examples of other Yuletide greenery with a strong pagan past. The red berries of the holly remind us of the blood sacrifices carried out in ancient paganism to fertilise the land, while its prickly leaves remind us it is a 'male' plant sacred to the Horned God and Old Father Christmas. Holly is regarded as a good luck plant and a bush placed outside the front door will attract good fortune and protect the house from fire, lightning and the Evil Eye. On no account should holly be burnt or brought into the house in the summer or bad luck will follow. It is definitely a plant of the god of the winter.

In contrast, ivy has always been regarded as a 'female' plant. It was a symbol of fertility and if it grows on the walls of a house it will protect the occupants from evil. If it withers and dies then disaster will befall the household and in Welsh folklore this signifies the imminent loss of the property to another family. Ivy became very popular in the 17th century and its berries were crushed and steeped in vinegar as a remedy for the plague.

The traditional Christmas Tree was allegedly introduced into this country by Prince Albert in 1841. It had been widely known on the Continent since at least the 17th century and probably much earlier. Decorated trees were a prominent feature of the Saturnalia and ancient Northern European midwinter rites. It is recorded that the early Christian saint Boniface ordered that all the sacred oaks worshipped by the Germans should be cut down. This caused such an uproar that he replaced them with fir trees and this became the traditional Christmas Tree.

Before the introduction of electric lights candles were burnt on the tree to represent the light of the sun. The coloured baubles represent the seven classical planets or the nine

Dragging home the Yule Log on Christmas Eve

worlds in Norse mythology. Small gifts tied to the branches are symbols of prosperity and fertility, while the tinsel draped around the tree is the world serpent who in Northern belief encircles Midgard or Middle Earth. The fairy on the top is an image of the sun goddess, although sometimes she is replaced by a star. This is the North or Pole Star, around which the universe is said to revolve.

The 19th century introduction of the Christmas Tree eventually replaced the old English custom of the Kissing Bough. This was a double loop or spherical framework covered with evergreens and decorated with candles, ribbons and apples. Again this symbol would seem to date back to pagan times, and represents the light of the sun and the promise of eternal life at the darkest point of the year.

One Christmas Eve custom that has almost died out today is the Yule Log. This is a relic of the ancient fires lit by our Celtic and Norse ancestors to greet the rebirth of the sun at dawn on the winter solstice. The Yule Log was traditionally of ash or oak and was collected by the children from the woods in the afternoon. If you passed the Log you were required by custom to bow or raise your hat if you were wearing one. At the house it was decorated with sprigs of greenery and sprinkled with a libation of cider. In accordance with pagan ritual, the Yule Log was lit from a surviving remnant of the previous one. It was expected to burn for at least twelve hours and if large enough was relit each evening during the Twelve Days. In some areas it was kept until Candlemas Day, then relit and allowed to burn out.

The collection and burning of the Log was an important social event that was believed to bring good fortune to everyone associated with it. The ashes from the fire were often sprinkled on the fields to bring a good harvest or were used as magical charms to ward off evil and heal the sick. It was said that while the Yule Log burned, everyone within the house would be safe from harm, whether natural or supernatural in origin.

In Scotland a variation on the Yule Log was the ritual burning of the Cailleach or Old Hag on Christmas Eve. The men of the household were sent out to find a withered tree stump or twisted branch which they then carved into the

The Yule Log arrives

representation of an old woman. This represented the
female spirit of winter, the dark aspect of the Goddess. In
the evening the Cailleach was thrown on the fire, while the
family sat around it drinking whisky and telling bawdy
jokes or ghost stories. Sadly it seems that today the
ancient tradition of the Yule Log only survives in the ritual
eating of chocolate covered Swiss rolls decorated with
plastic robins and snowmen.

Burning the Yule Log was a rural pastime and in towns and
cities it was the Yule Candle that was substituted. These
were large coloured candles decorated with holly sprigs,
sparkling glitter and gold and silver paint. Traditionally it

25

was lit at bedtime on Christmas Eve and allowed to burn through the night. Sometimes it was lit every day for a short period through the holiday season. It was considered very unlucky if it blew out accidentally and only the head of the family could light or extinguish it. The remnants of the Yule Candle were kept as lucky charms or, in country districts where the practice was known, its wax was smeared on the plough blade to ensure good crops.

December 25th

Midnight on Christmas Eve was regarded as a strange and even sinister time. It was when the gates of the Other-world were open and the living could communicate with the dead. This may well explain why the Church decided to celebrate a Midnight Mass at this time, ostensibly to welcome the birth of Jesus. In rural Wales this special Mass was known as the plygain or 'cock crow' and was celebrated early on Christmas morning. It was especially for young people, who gathered the evening before at a local farm and sang, danced and played the harp until it was time to leave for the church. At Laugharne in Carmarthenshire, until the wartime 'black-out' ended the practice, the boys of the village used to escort the vicar to Mass carrying blazing torches. Curtis (1880) says: 'It is thought this originated out of the superstitious rites of the heathen Britons.'

The highlight of Christmas Day, past or present, is the traditional lunch or dinner. The eating of turkey seems to have been a fairly modern innovation and was reintroduced into this country by American servicemen during the First World War, although it had been known during Tudor times. Goose and duck were the favoured Christmas fare

'Sweeping bad luck' onto the Christmas Night fire

for our ancestors and it is interesting that the goose is a symbol and sacred bird of the winter goddess Holle or Holda. In some parts of the country the medieval custom of serving a boar's head was reserved for Christmas Day.

This dates back to the sacrifice of boars in Norse religion, for the animal was sacred to the ithyphallic god of fertility and the harvest, Frey. In the Middle Ages the grand entrance of the boar's head into the banqueting hall was an amazing spectacle. It was carried in on a huge silver platter, garlanded with bay leaves and rosemary and with a large apple stuffed in its mouth. The beast was accompanied by playing minstrels and a jester, while behind it followed a train of servants carrying other dishes laden with rich Christmas food.

The Boar's Head Ceremony still takes place at Queen's College, Oxford where it is said to date from the 14th century. Its origins are explained in a bizarre tale about a scholar who encountered a wild boar while out for a stroll. As he was unarmed he allegedly choked it to death by thrusting a rolled up manuscript of the writings of the Greek philosophers down its throat! In reality this ceremony is more likely to be a memory of the sacrificial rites of Frey, who was sometimes represented in the shape of a boar.

Plum pudding is another Christmas favourite with pagan undertones. It is said to have been the chosen diet of the Irish god of fertility, Dagda the Good, who like Frey boasted an enormous penis and carried a club like Old Father Christmas. Dagda was the proud owner of a magical cauldron with the power to regenerate the dead and in this sacred vessel he cooked a special porridge made of corn and fruit. The act of setting the Christmas pudding alight with brandy could be the relic of a previous fire ritual. Especially as once alight it resembles the blazing disc of the sun.

Once Christmas dinner has been consumed and the diners have rested, it is time for party games. The charades, endless games of Trivial Pursuit and the latest computer game which make up the modern Christmas Day afternoon also have their origins in ancient rites. We have already seen how the Twelve Days of Yule were under the control of the Lord of Misrule. Well, he was also in charge of the guisers; bands of men dressed in masks, ragged clothes and animal costumes. It was the dances and plays performed by the guisers - from whom we get the English slang term 'geezer', meaning a funny or strange old man - that have survived to become the tradition of party games at the modern Christmas.

Bringing in the Boar's head

The mumming or mummer's plays performed by the guisers traditionally occurred during the Christmas holiday period, although they were a winter feature and could be performed any time between Hallowe'en and Easter. Boxing Day and Twelfth Night were special dates for their performance. While 'guiser' or 'guising' means to dress up, hence disguise, the word 'mummer' probably means 'mask' or 'masker'. The common elements in the mumming plays was that the actors wore masks and ragged clothes decorated with ribbons or strips of paper. The leading mummer or guiser usually wore a special cap or head dress made of rabbit or fox skin. Sometimes the whole skin was used with the face attached, alternatively he wore a top hat decorated with wild flowers or holly.

The main characters in the plays include St George, the Lady, the Fool, the Dame, the Knight, the Bride and the Doctor. In some versions the players were known collectively as 'Molly's Children', indicating possible Goddess worship links. Sometimes Old Father Christmas would put in an appearance. St George features because he was the patron saint of medieval England and is also a, heavily disguised, version of the Green Man, the old god of the witches in his summery aspect. As in traditional panto, the text of the plays often alluded to historical characters and popular heroes, who were added or deleted according to fashionable opinion of the day. These included personalities as diverse as Lord Nelson, Wellington and Napoleon.

The format of the mumming plays follows a standard format reflecting its pagan origins. They usually involve a ritual combat between two champions or a hero and a villain. This leads to the stage death of one of the combatants, who is then revived from the dead by a wonder-working (shaman type) figure called the Doctor. Alex Helm (1981) has described the mumming plays as 'A man's seasonal festival designed to promote fertility' and it has obvious connections with Morris dancing, which uses some of the same folk characters.

The Christmas period was also celebrated by the wearing of various animal masks. One English example which survived until comparatively recently was the so-called Christmas Bull. This strange creature was found mostly in

THE DORSET OOSER

The Dorset Ooser

the West Country, especially in the counties of Gloucestershire, Wiltshire and Dorset. In the latter it was known as the Ooser, while in parts of Wiltshire it was called the Wooset. Folklorists have traced this name back to the medieval woodwoses, Wild Men or Green Men, believed to be spirits that haunted the forest. The bull was also the sacred animal of the sun god worshipped in Celtic and Bronze Age times.

The famous Dorset Ooser was a mask carved from a solid block of wood, except that the lower jaw was hinged so it could snap open and shut. The features were semi-human with real bull's horns attached to the head. This ritual mask was in annual use until the 1890s when it mysteriously vanished from the possession of a family in the Dorset village of Melbury Osmond. A few years ago the tradition of the Ooser was revived in the Dorset hamlet of

Cerne Abbas, famous for its phallic giant hill figure which, according to latest research, may have been carved to represent a local Celtic horned god.

More generally the Christmas Bull was a hollowed out head of a bull carved from wood, with glass eyes and attached to a pole. Its human operator hid beneath a 'body' made of sacking or a white cloth. In some cases this was the actual hide of a cow or bull. The Bull, accompanied by its retinue, travelled around the villages, singing carols outside each cottage and farm. When the unsuspecting householder opened the door the Bull charged in and chased everyone, especially the women, from room to room. He could only be placated by feeding its attendants mince pies and giving them beer to drink.

A more sedate, if no less sinister, version of the Christmas Bull is the Mari Llwyd, or Grey Mare, who is still to be found in south Wales. The Christian version of her origins links her with Mary and Joseph visiting each inn with a donkey, but it is more likely that the tradition dates back to the Celtic worship of the horse goddess Epona in south Wales or even Odin's magical steed introduced by the Vikings who raided and colonised West and south Wales. It is interesting to note that in Norse magic a horse's skull mounted on a pole carved with runes was used in cursing and hexing rites.

The Mari consists of a horse's skull with a loose jawbone that could open and shut and pieces of glass for the eyes. This is mounted on a five foot pole and decorated with ribbons. The pole is then draped with a white sheet underneath which the operator crouches. In the old days she was accompanied by a man known as the Serjeant-at-Arms, a Fiddler called the Merry Man and sometimes a male odd couple called Punch and Judy. The latter was sometimes called the Old Woman (the Hag Goddess?) and carried a broom. All these attendants blacked their faces so they could not be recognised.

At dusk the Mari sets out on its journey around the parish and usually does not end its wanderings until midnight. At each house the Fiddler played a traditional tune while the others sang a song to which the people inside had to respond to. Today the exchange is in the form of insults, with the people refusing entry because the Mari's breath smells or there is no room in the house for it or no food for the guisers. After this repartee the Mari is allowed in and proceeds to chase the women, biting them on the bottom and generally misbehaving, while the attendants help themselves to mince pies, bara brith and cans of beer.

An English version of the Mari was the Hooden Horse of Kent, first mentioned in 1731. The last recorded performance by the Horse was in 1908, before it was revived in 1956. In the 1900s the Horse was a painted wooden head on a four foot pole. This was covered with sacking underneath which the operator crouched. The Horse's mane was made from plaited ribbons or real horsehair and it had a moveable jaw with 'teeth' made from nails. In addition to the Hoodener, or operator, the Horse was accompanied by a Groom or Waggoner with a whip, a Jockey and a man-woman called Molly, who swept in front of the procession with a besom. They all had black faces and rang handbells as they went from house to house singing carols.

There are several different versions of the origin of the Hooden Horse's name. These include the wooden horse, Woden's horse, the hooded horse and Robin Hood's horse.

Woden or Odin was often called 'the Hooded One' or 'The Masked One', while Robin Hood is a form of the witch god and is connected to Woden through Herne the Hunter. Both the Mari and the Hooden Horse, together with the Padstow 'Oss and Minehead Horse we shall describe later, belong to a category of ritual animal disguises known as hobby horses.

The word 'hobby' is first recorded in the late 14th century as a type of horse. The Middle English 'hobyn' and 'hoby' are related to the nicknames of Robin, Robbie and Dobbin used for carthorses. Hobby may originate from the Dutch 'hoppe' and in common usage meant a small, ambling horse with a shorn mane. By Tudor times the 'hobby horse' had become associated with the Morris and was a slang word for a fool, jester or prostitute. By the 16th and 17th centuries it had developed into a child's toy with a horse head on a stick. Later 18th and 19th centuries usage associates it with the wooden horses on fairground merry-go-rounds and with rocking horses. In 18th century brothels a variant of the hobby horse was in the shape of a rooster with a beak in the shape of a phallus that lay along its back. This was then 'ridden' like a rocking horse by women to obtain sexual pleasure.

December 26th

The day after Christmas is the feast of St Stephen, although today it is more generally known as Boxing Day. This name comes from the old custom of opening small boxes in which alms had been collected during the year and distributing them to the poor. Often these gift boxes were in the form of earthenware pigs with a slot at the top and they had to be broken, or symbolically sacrificed, to release the contents. These 'piggy banks' have an obvious connection with the sacred boars of the Norse god Frey, god of fertility and prosperity. It is therefore not surprising to find that in the Christian version St Stephen was employed in the kitchens of King Herod's palace where he was responsible for preparing the boar's head.

An unusual and cruel folk rite carried out on St Stephen's Day was 'Hunting the Wren'. This practice, dating back to druidic times, was observed in the former Celtic regions of Ireland, the Isle of Man, Wales and parts of East Anglia. A wren was hunted down, killed and then given a mock

Procession of the Wren Boys - Boxing Day in Wales

funeral during which it was carried through the streets in a specially built 'wren house'. Sometimes it was crucified on a pole so that it appeared to be flying.

The person who killed the wren was treated like royalty and it was thought to be an act that brought good luck throughout the coming year. All the 'wren boys' had blackened faces and at the end of the procession the bird was laid to rest in the churchyard. Before it was buried, the feathers were removed and sold as lucky charms.

As the dead bird was paraded through the streets the boys accompanying it sang the 'Wren Song', with its references to 'hunting the wren for Robin the Bobbin'. In the nursery rhyme Robin the Bobbin is a character with an enormous appetite that could not be satisfied. In another version he shoots his brother with a bow and arrow. This 'brother' has been identified by folklorists as either the wren killed on Boxing Day or the hero of another nursery rhyme, Who Killed Cock Robin?

Cock Robin represents the divine king who is sacrificed to the Goddess after his seven year reign to bring fertility to the land. The Celtic writer Lewis Spence identified Robin the Bobbin with the solar god Bel or Belinus, while Stewart (1977) has suggested that references in the song to a 'brass cauldron' may be linked with ancient sacrificial rites. Both the Irish god Dagda and the Welsh witch-goddess Ceridwen owned famous cauldrons associated with fertility, death, rebirth, spiritual transformation and the underworld. In Wales the wren, despite its small size, is known as 'the King of the Birds' and the 'druid's bird' and is said to always nest in the sacred oak tree.

As attitudes changed the cruelty of the wren hunt was modified. On the Isle of Man it was replaced by a group of boys carrying a garland decorated with leaves and flowers on a pole. They still sang the famous Wren's Song and collected money from passers-by. In Scotland the wren was captured, decorated with ribbons and then released. In West Wales the bird was briefly imprisoned in a glass box or cage and people were invited to donate money for the release of 'the smallest who is yet king' In Ireland, where the poor bird had been crucified, it was replaced by a potato carved in the shape of a bird and covered with feathers.

Another curious custom performed on Boxing Day in Wales was linked with the martyrdom of Stephen. It was called Holly Beating and was carried out by gangs of young boys who roamed the streets beating working class women and domestic servants with holly sprigs on their upper arms until they bled. This unpleasant blood-letting rite was banned by law in the 1850s, but survived in the Gower area of south Wales, where it was called 'Holming', until the 1880s. In Montgomeryshire the last person who got up on Boxing Day was thrashed with holly and had to act as the family's slave until New Year's Eve.

Holming was related to the common practice of bleeding livestock, especially horses, on St Stephen's Day. An 18th century writer on the subject gave the broad hint that it had to do with the waxing of the sun after the winter solstice. The farmers said that they did it because blood-letting was beneficial to the health of the animals. This idea, and the sadistic Holly Beating custom, can be traced back to the ritual blood sacrifices made at the solstice in pre-Christian times in connection with seed sowing and to protect the animals from summer diseases.

December 31st

The ancient Celts began their New Year on November 1st, known as Samhain or 'summer's end'. In the Christian calendar until 1600 the New Year coincided with the vernal equinox and was celebrated on March 25th, Lady's Day. It was not until 1752, when the new Gregorian calendar was introduced, that the Church accepted January 1st as New Year's Day. The common people had celebrated it on that date and many of the old customs and rites of the midwinter festival had become mingled with the celebration of the New Year.

In Scotland, where Hogmanay was more important then Christmas, people gathered at the kirk or church at midnight on New Year's Eve. As many pre-Reformation churches were erected on pagan sites this custom probably dates back to that period. Some evidence for this is provided by the inhabitants of the Orkneys who met at a local stone circle to greet the New Year.

In the 18th century the cleric on Ronaldsay reported seeing fifty people dancing around a standing stone on New Year's Eve. As time passed such blatantly heathen observances were replaced by drunken revellers gathering in the market square to hear the town clock strike midnight.

The orgiastic rituals that once marked the beginning of the year survived in a sublimated form as late as the last century. These included the custom of 'kissing for good luck' which was popular, especially among the male population, in the early hours of New Year's Day. It was decreed that any woman who was out on the streets after midnight could not refuse to be kissed by any man she encountered. The sacred meal once eaten to celebrate the

New Year also survived in the oat cakes and whisky flavoured ale used to toast the midnight bells.

The midwinter bonfires lit by our Norse ancestors at the solstice are remembered in the folk ceremony known as tar barrelling. At Allendale in Northumbria, Viking country, just before midnight on New Year's Eve, men carry blazing tar barrels through the streets. As midnight strikes they are heaped into a bonfire in the town square. A similar ceremony, known as Burning the Old Year Out, was celebrated at Biggar on Strathclyde. The bonfire was prepared as early as November and money for its materials was collected by carol-singing guisers. The Yule Fire, as it is sometimes called, was set alight within sight of a hill said to have been used for druidic worship.

At Newton-Stewart in Gaily a torchlight procession took place until the outbreak of the First World War. A local Tar Barrel Association was formed and became expert in obtaining materials from local farms. While people were allowed to defend themselves from raids or try and retrieve their property from its secret hiding places, the police seldom intervened. On New Year's Eve the Association members rode through the streets on horses brandishing their torches. This mounted procession was led by a pipe band in full Highland regalia and culminated in a huge bonfire of tar barrels that burnt until dawn.

At Stonehaven in Kincardineshire the ancient festival of 'fireballing' was revived in the middle of the last century. This folk ritual was designed to drive away evil and attract good luck. The actual fireballs are made of wood shavings and rags soaked in paraffin and tar. Each of the balls is encased in wire netting and at the stroke of midnight the participants light them and then whirl them around their heads. This is supposed to keep away witches who might be flying overhead on their broomsticks.

Another New Year custom with pagan overtones was the Procession of the Hogmanay Bull. The hide of the Bull, complete with horns, hooves and tail attached, was stored in the farmhouse attic or in the rafters of the barn until it was needed. One of the farm workers dressed up in the costume while others armed themselves with staves covered in strips of sheepskin. Shortly before midnight on New Year's Eve the Bull and its attendants set out around the neighbouring farms and crofts.

At each place the hide of the Bull was beaten with the sticks to make a noise like a drum and a traditional song was sung. The Procession then circled the house deosil, or sunways, beating their staves on the walls. The Bull was then invited in and its tail was singed in the fire and all present inhaled the smoke. This odd practice apparently protected the household from harm during the coming year. On a symbolic level they were partaking of the Bull's essence and in earlier times a real bull would have been sacrificed and eaten.

Once the ritual was over the party were given food and drink as a reward. Before leaving they processed around the inside of the house singing a charm which granted good fortune. Dire consequences followed if by any chance the Bull was not invited in or made welcome. Then the Procession marched widdershins, or anti-clockwise, around the house and a small cairn of stones was built. The Bull then called down a curse on the family and he invoked all cats, badgers, ravens and foxes to cause the household harm during the year.

January 1st

The most important custom performed in the early hours of New Year is 'first footing'. The actual 'first footer' is the first stranger or member of the household who crosses the threshold after midnight. His or her physical appearance was very important for it was an omen of the kind of year the family could expect. Hunchbacked, squinty-eyed, lame or deformed people were a bad sign. Red haired people or those wearing green were also unlucky as these were the Devil's colours. In the North Country blond men were shunned as they reminded people of the Viking invaders of yesteryear. Immoral folk, the elderly, cross-eyed, flat-footed and miserly people were also omens of misfortune. Anyone carrying a knife, begging or in black (mourning) clothes would be forbidden entry.

To remove any risk or chance of mishap, a special ritual was devised using a specially selected person with the right qualities and therefore Fate was cheated. Traditionally the first footer should be young, tall, dark and handsome if male, and young, fair and beautiful if female. In some parts of England women of any kind were regarded as unlucky and female visitors were discouraged. Children of all types were welcomed.

The first footer must never come empty-handed, or the family will fall into poverty. Acceptable gifts were whisky, bread, salt, a silver coin, an apple or a lump of coal or a log for the fire. In rural areas the first footer brought corn for a good harvest and in fishing villages a herring or mackerel. All these gifts are folk memories of the sacrificial offerings made to the Old Gods and the first footer represents the priest or shaman who invoked the divine forces on behalf of the worshippers.

This is underlined strongly in the instances where the first footer brings a gift of evergreens into the house. Sometimes it is a sprig of the sacred mistletoe which is then placed on the mantelpiece over the hearth - the symbolic centre of the household. In most cases the first footer will not speak until he or she has walked over and stirred (blessed) the fire. Then, in the manner of a priest, they turn and wish the assembled family a happy and prosperous New Year. Once the gifts had been handed over it was then essential that the visitor was quickly offered food and drink or the luck would vanish. Doom would follow if the first footer was not treated properly or insulted.

The next important New Year custom was the drawing of the first water from the well or river at dawn. Anyone chosen to do this was blessed with good luck for the rest of the year. If it was an unmarried woman she would wed before the next Christmas. Farmers often gave this first water to their cows to increase their milk and any not used was bottled and used as 'holy water' to ward off evil.

If the person drawing the water did not throw a posy of flowers into the well or river this was regarded as bad luck. In Radnorshire country folk 'dressed' the wells with sprigs of box and brewed a special tea from the first water as a health tonic. It goes almost without saying that these customs date back to pre-Christian water worship at sacred springs.

Herefordshire farmers used to carry out a New Year fire ritual at dawn called Burning the Bush. This survived until the 1900s and its purpose was to stop the wheat becoming infected with the fungus known locally as 'smut'. Farmworkers arose early and carried the Bush, a ball of hawthorn twigs made the previous year and hung in the kitchen 'for luck', to the fields. It was then set alight and carried around the boundaries until it burnt out. Afterwards a new Bush was made for the next year, soaked in cider and singed in the flames from the old one to blacken the twigs. The ceremony ended with the celebrants toasting the New Year in with jugs of cider and returning to the farmhouse for a mammoth breakfast of eggs, bacon, sausages and mushrooms.

In Wales the first calf to be born in the New Year was presented with a sprig of mistletoe. In Cardiff in the 19th century children visited their parents bedrooms early on New Years morning and gave them an apple stuck with pieces of oat and a sprig of rosemary. The apple was said to represent the earth, the oats the life which sprung from it now that midwinter was passed and the greenery was the promise of an early spring.

January 5th

Twelfth Night is the eve of Epiphany in the Christian calendar, which commemorates the presentation of their gifts by the three Magi, astrologers or Wise Men to the baby Jesus. In the Gregorian calendar it was Old Christmas Eve and it is still celebrated as such in the Eastern Orthodox Church.

The evening of January 5th marked the semi-official end of the Twelve Days when the Christmas decorations were taken down, although in some remote country districts they were kept until Candlemas. Very little work was carried out during the Twelve Days and Welsh farmers brought the plough into the house and placed it under the kitchen table until the holiday was over. So it was not forgotten during this rest libations of beer were poured over it at frequent intervals.

Twelfth Night was the time for more fire rituals to signify that the midwinter point had been passed and the sun was rising in the sky from now on. Herefordshire, Gloucestershire and Worcestershire farm workers went out into the fields at dusk and lit twelve bonfires in a circle with a smaller one in the centre. They then toasted their master in cider or beer and asked for a good year on the land. After a large supper they then visited the byres, sang songs to the livestock and prayed for their health. A plum cake was offered to the best bull and placed on his horns. If he tossed it backward then a bad harvest could be expected, but if he tossed it forward all would be well.

Although the thirteen bonfires were said to represent Jesus and his disciples, it is tempting to see them as the thirteen moons of the year or the signs of the Zodiac with the sun in the centre. Especially as sometimes they called the central fire the Virgin Mary or the Old Witch. This unique custom, embracing fire worship, prayers for a good harvest and fine weather, offerings to bulls and divination, would appear to date back to before the introduction of Christianity.

January 6th

By the Julian calendar introduced in Europe in 1582 and in Britain in 1752, Twelfth Day was Old Christmas Day and in some remote areas it was still observed as such for years after the changeover. As late as 1850 Herefordshire folk held special Christmas services on this day and older people carried this on until the 1930s. For others this was the day when the ashes of the Yule Log were removed and either stored for magical purposes or scattered on the fields.

In medieval times a temporary version of the Lord of Misrule was elected for this day to rule over the final fling of the Yuletide revels. He was known as the King of the Bean and was selected by a form of divination dating back to the dark days of human sacrifice. Cakes were made and into one was baked a bean. Whoever chose this special cake was elected as the king for a day. This custom was popular at court, in colleges and even religious houses until the 18th century calendar reform when it suddenly stopped.

The Haxey Hood game takes place usually around Old Christmas Day and it also has a powerful symbolism of human sacrifice. The game takes place in the village of Haxey in Lincolnshire and begins in the afternoon when the Fool, clad in trousers decorated with red patches and with his face blotched with soot and red ochre, processes with his twelve Boggans along the main street. They stop on the green in front of the church and the Fool carries a whip which he playfully hits bystanders with and demands kisses from any woman he fancies along the way.

The celebrant of the ritual is the Lord of the Hood, who carries a ceremonial wand made of thirteen willow sticks. He also wears a red coat and a top hat wreathed in flowers. Some of the Boggans, led by the Chief Boggan, wear red jerseys.

When this merry band reach the church the Fool gives a short speech from a stone which was once part of a cross outside the churchyard. He welcomes everyone to the game and invites those interested to participate. During this speech the Fool makes cryptic references to the killing of two bulls and a half and tells the crowd that the other half is still running around the field and can be caught if required.

While the Fool is still explaining the rules of the game, a small fire is lit behind him using damp straw so that he soon becomes obscured in thick smoke. This is in fact a modification of an even stranger practice, when the Fool was 'smoked' by being tied to a rope and swung back and forth over a fire. After a near fatality this dangerous practice was stopped.

Once he has finished his speech, the Fool leads the assembly up the hill to a piece of wasteground measuring about half an acre where the game begins The basic idea is to get a small 'hood', made of canvas and tied with ribbons, across the parish boundary and into the own player's village while eluding the Boggans and other players. If a Boggan touches the hood it is considered to be dead and handed back to the Lord. Successful players are allowed to keep their hoods.

When all the small hoods have been won, the real game starts. This is known as the Sway and the Sway Hood is a piece of rope some two feet long covered with leather. Whoever catches it is immediately surrounded and can only be pushed or swayed towards one of three public houses in the area. This can take several hours as the Sway Hood is wrestled from group to group. Today the Hood remains in the possession of the landlord of the pub it reaches, but in former years it was ritually roasted over a fire and libated with ale.

Allegedly the origins of the game go back to the 13th century when Lady Mowbray was out riding and her hood was blown away in the wind. Thirteen farmworkers chased after it, but the one who caught it was so shy he would not return it to the lady. For this reason the others nicknamed him the Fool. One of the others did return it and in gratitude the lady of the manor gave the workers thirteen acres of land if they promised to re-enact the chase for her hood every year as a game.

Despite this charming fairy tale the explicit symbolism of the Haxey Hood game with its Fool given the freedom to roam the streets whipping people and kissing women, the widespread use of red in the players' clothing, the Lord's willow wand, the thirteen Boggans and the ritual hanging above a fire suggest the type of sacrificial rite once common around this time of year. It has been said that originally the Hood was the dried pizzle or penis of a bull.

Plough Monday

In the rural calendar the new agricultural year began on the first Monday after Twelfth Day and this was commonly called Plough Monday, because it was when the winter ploughing was supposed to begin. In practice very little work was attempted on this special day and instead a decorated plough was dragged around the fields by young people dressed up as goblins and witches. Often there was also a she-male, a man dressed in women's clothing, who was called Molly, Betsy or Bessie.

Sometimes the plough was dragged through the streets of the village while its bearers begged for money. Anyone who refused was in danger of having their garden ploughed up so few did. Before the Reformation the money collected was used to finance the burning of a large candle, known as the

Plough Monday Procession - 18th Century, with Betsy and
Fool

Plough Light, on the church altar. This ensured good
weather for the ploughing, a bumper harvest and protected
the workers from sickness or injury. After the 16th century
the money was handed to the churchwarden for the parish
fund. These semi-pagan customs died out with the
increasing mechanisation of the farming industry, but still
survive today in the annual service of 'Blessing the Plough'.

January 17th

This date marks the wassailing of the cider orchards in the
West Country to produce a good crop of cider apples in the
autumn. The word 'wassail' comes from the Norse 'wes

'Sow the seeds and scatter'

hail', the Old English 'wes hall' and the medieval English 'waes hael', meaning 'good health', 'good cheer' or 'be whole'. This was a salutation made at New Year when lambswool, a potent mix of mulled ale, herbs and honey dating from Saxon times, was served in ornately decorated wassailing bowls.

On the night of January 17th, which was known as Old Twelfth Night, the wassailers visit the cider orchards carrying shotguns, hunting horns and buckets brimming with cider. The cider was poured over the roots of the trees, the shotguns blasted into the branches and the horns are blown to ward off evil. Sometimes the trees are beaten with sticks to stimulate growth. Such rituals are performed with serious intent and in January 1994 the managing director of a Herefordshire cider company, resplendent in a top hat decorated with holly and ivy, told a television interviewer that the ceremony was essential if a commercial crop was to be produced each year.

Santa Claus - the modern version of Old Father
Christmas and Odin/Woden

Chapter Three

Candlemas to Easter

In Celtic times the beginning of February was the fire festival of Imbolc, dedicated to the goddess Brigid or Brighid. She was the daughter of our old friend Dagda and she has variously been linked with the Morrigan, Dana and Brigantia. Brigid, whose name means 'bright' or 'exalted' was Christianised as St Bride or St Bridget and was said to have been the Virgin Mary's midwife and the wet nurse of Jesus. Bride or Brigid appears in triple form and was the patron of poetry, smithcraft, healing, childbirth, holy wells and beacon fires. At Kildare in Ireland a sacred fire was kept burning in her name by nine nuns until the Catholic Church banned it. Some authorities believe that Brigid was a solar goddess, hence the importance of her festival at a time when the sun is beginning to wax towards the spring.

In Celtic mythology the winter months were ruled from Hallowe'en to Candlemas by the Cailleach or Old Hag, the goddess of winter and darkness. One Scottish folk tale says she keeps Bride imprisoned during the cold winter until she is rescued by Aengus, the white god of light, and the spring begins. In another legend, Bride is another form of the Hag and on Imbolc Eve the Caillecah goes to the Island of Youth

St Brigid - Celtic saint and sun goddess

and drinks from its well. She is then transformed into the spring goddess whose touch turns the grass green and makes the snowdrops bloom.

February 1st

Imbolc or Imbolg, meaning 'ewe's milk', was on this day but gradually has become merged with Candlemas on February 2nd, the Feast of the Purification of the Virgin Mary. In the Highlands, and on some of the Scottish islands, young women celebrated Imbolc by fashioning a female image from a sheaf of wheat. This was decorated with shells,

St Bride's Doll

snowdrops and jewellry and a special crystal was placed over the heart of the figure. The image was then carried from house to house and every family had to make an offering of a shell, crystal or flower which was added to its finery. At the end of the processing the Bride was taken to one house and there the men were allowed to pay homage.

The older women made a bed or cradle for the Bride image and she was placed into it. Next to this bed was positioned a small straight wand made of birch, willow or some other sacred 'feminine' wood. Incense was burnt on the hearth and the next morning the ashes were carefully examined for traces of footprints to see if Bride had visited during the night. Special Brigid crosses were also made from rushes

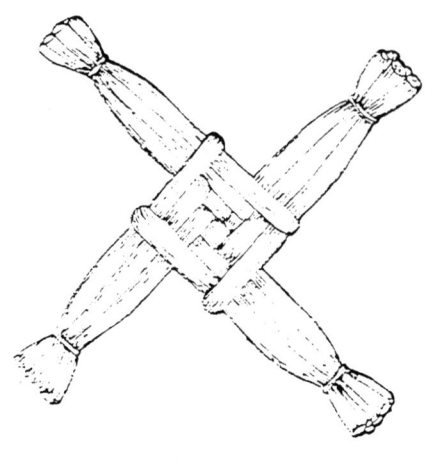

St Bride's Cross

in the form of Celtic crosses, diamond shapes with triple arms or even in the form of swastikas or solar crosses.

St Bride's Day was also associated with the first stirrings from hibernation of our native snakes, the adder and viper. In Scotland a traditional chant was sung on Imbolc morning as follows:

Today is the day of Bride,
The serpent shall come from the hole,
The queen will come from the mound,
I will not molest the serpent,
The serpent will not molest me

This symbolises the return of the spring goddess after the winter and her re-emergence from the underworld, the Hollow Hill or mound.

February 2nd

As we have seen this was Candlemas and as the name suggests it was when the new candles to be used in church were blessed on the high altar. For this reason Candlemas is sometimes called the Festival of Lights and it marked the return of the virgin to the temple in Jerusalem to be purified after childbirth. In Roman times people processed through the streets with torches and candles in honour of Februa, the mother of the god of agriculture and war, Mars. An early Pope banned this pagan ritual and decreed that in future her worshippers should come to church and light a candle to the Virgin Mary.

Candlemas was an important quarter day in the agricultural calendar and its weather was seen as an omen of the spring to come. It was said that if the day dawned bright and clear then cold weather would follow shortly. If on Candlemas Day 'the thorns hang adrop' there will be a good crop of peas and that could only happen if there was an early, warm spring. This weather lore obviously links the day with the spring goddess who brings good weather.

February 14th

St Valentine's Day, named after an obscure saint who in reality may have been a Gnostic heretic who preached free love. The festival dates back to the Roman Lupercalia on February 15th in honour of the goat-foot god Pan, the supreme mother goddess Juno and the she-wolf who suckled Remus and Romulus. On this day the young men of Rome ran naked through the streets dressed only in wolf skins whipping any women they met. It was also the festival of Persephone, goddess of the underworld, and her emergence into the world in spring to join her mother, the corn goddess Demeter.

A popular feature of the Lupercalia was a sexual lottery. Women placed their names on slips of paper in a box and these were drawn at random by men who accepted them as lovers. This survived into Christian times with both sexes participating. The slips of paper were called valentines, after the saint, and eventually were transformed into greeting cards sent to lovers or would-be lovers.

Shrove Tuesday

A moveable Christian festival that usually falls near Valentine's Day. Today it is generally known as Pancake Day, but in the old days it was a rowdy festival characterised by cock fights, horse racing, dancing and drunken brawls. In 1868 it is recorded as Blackamoor Night, when little boys blacked their faces and went from door to door begging for sweets.

In the north-east of England and on the Scottish Border it was Bannock Night and only pancakes and milk gruel were eaten. Before cooking the bannocks the eggs were dropped into a glass of cold water and the future divined from the shape they formed.

The last cake cooked, known as the dumb cake, was used for divining by adding symbolic objects to it such as a thimble, coin or ring symbolising types of husband. The cake was cut up and pieces were then selected from the cook's apron and interpreted.

Cornish folk held a semi-pagan festival around this time called Nicky Nan Night. This was usually on the Monday before Shrove Tuesday and it was a time when the young men roamed the streets causing mayhem and mischief. The festival featured the carrying in procession of a burning straw figure, possibly representing Joan the Wad, the Queen of the Piskies or Pixies, and a ritual meal of pea soup. On Shrove Tuesday itself the inhabitants of Penzance went out to collect shellfish on the beach. Folklorists believe this custom may be a relic of a former pagan ritual of worshipping the Great Mother Goddess, or a local sea goddess.

March 21st/22nd

The vernal or spring equinox is regarded in many rural communities as the official first day of spring. In the northern hemisphere its date can be either the 20th, 21st or 22nd according to the leap year cycle. The spring and autumn equinoxes are the two days in the year when the hours of day and night are equal. The vernal equinox is also the day when the sun enters the Zodiac sign of Aries.

As the days begin to get longer and the sun rises in the sky there comes the almost compulsive and universal urge to 'spring clean', throwing out all the unwanted things collected during the dark season, be they physical objects, bad habits or states of mind. It is a time for changing the furniture around, for changes in the house are symbolic of changes in the outside world and in your self.

Easter

This is another of the Christian moveable festivals and it remains so despite the attempts to pass legislation to fix it on the same weekend every year. The formula used to calculate the date is a complicated one based on the timing of the Jewish Passover. The early Church in fact celebrated the festival at the same time as the Passover until the Roman Church forced the Celtic Christians to accept their date. Basically, Easter Sunday is the first Sunday after the full moon that follows the spring equinox. It can therefore either be celebrated in late March or in April.

Originally Easter marked the early spring festival of the pagan peoples of ancient Europe. This is proved by the many popular Easter symbols, such as the Easter Bunny, Easter Eggs and Hot Cross Buns, that have been blatantly borrowed from pre-Christian sources. The very name Easter derives from the Saxon goddess Eostre or Oestara, who ruled over the spring and the dawn. Easter refers not only to the dawn or birth of a new day, but also a new year starting at the spring equinox with its symbolism of rebirth, revival and resurrection.

Variants of the name Eostre can be found in German, Lithuanian, Hindu and Latin. In Greek mythology she was known as Aurora and is described as the daughter of a Titan, or giant, and the mother of the four winds. As the morning star she is depicted rising out of the east every day bringing light to the world and is a typical Northern European sun goddess. Her mother was allegedly Jord, the ancient Germanic earth goddess, and as late as the 19th century stone altars were set up in rural parts of Germany to honour this goddess. These altars were known as Easter Stones and were decorated with wild flowers by the young people, who lit fires and danced around them to celebrate the dawn on Easter Day. This practice was carried on despite the wrath of the priests, who condemned such folk rites as devil worship.

This association between Easter and the solar goddess of the dawn appears to survive in a curious piece of folklore that claims that at dawn on Easter Sunday the sun dances for joy in celebration of the rising of Christ from the tomb. In 1906 a correspondent in a Herefordshire newspaper said she always believed this was a fallacy, until she actually witnessed this event on Easter Day of that year.

The Easter Bunny was originally the hare, the sacred animal of Eostre and a symbol of the moon in cultures worldwide. The moon hare is supposed to have laid the Cosmic Egg from which all life was hatched and this has become the chocolate eggs we eat today in their millions. Popular country lore said that the hare's gestation period was twenty eight days, comparable with the moons monthly cycle. It was also commonly believed that hares were androgynous and changed gender every year.

Hunting hares was an important folk ritual in bygone days at Easter time. Hare-coursing meetings are still held around the Easter weekend despite the brave attempts by animal welfare activists to stop this cruel 'sport'. Originally the hunt was for the eggs the hare was supposed to have laid and then it was for the animal itself. Hare pie was a traditional Easter dish, although some country people still believed in the old pagan taboo that it was unlucky to kill or eat a hare.

Hunting the hare and the Hare Pie Scramble were both customs followed on Easter Monday in Leicestershire as late as the 18th century. The hunt took place at the significantly named Black Annis' Bower. Black Annis was a Celtic form of the Hag Goddess who rules winter and she could take the form of a cat or hare. Legends and fairy tales about old witches who lived in woods with a black cat and could transform themselves into hares are often folk memories of the Hag Goddess, or her priestesses.

The actual hunt featured a pack of hounds who chased the tail of a dead cat or the skin of a hare. The Hare Pie Scramble in Hallaton (Holy Town) involved two pies, a large quantity of ale, two dozen loaves and a stuffed hare on a pole. A procession was led to a nearby hillock where the bread was thrown to the crowd, the beer distributed and everyone scrambled for a piece of pie. Traditionally this was never eaten, but thrown at other members of the crowd and spectators.

In many areas of Britain, and in Europe, the hare was also one of the animal forms taken by the Corn Spirit who fertilised the fields in the spring. At harvest time the last sheaf of corn was called the Corn Hare and when it was cut, always with a sickle, this was called 'Killing the Hare'. The worker who was responsible for the deed had to make a sacrificial offering of 'hare's blood', or brandy to the other workers.

Herefordshire families used to go out into the fields on Easter Sunday to call on the Corn Spirit for a good harvest. They sat down to a meal of plum cake and cider and solemnly poured a libation and buried a piece of cake while saying prayers for the farmer and a good crop. They then joined hands and danced across the field.

Eating Hot Cross Buns on Good Friday is another pagan relic. They originate in the special cakes baked in classical times as sacrificial offerings to the moon goddess Diana. The cakes were marked with an equal-armed cross to divide them into the four lunar quarters. These were then broken up into pieces and buried at the nearest crossroads as an offering to the goddess. In post-Christian times the remains of uneaten Hot Cross Buns were often preserved and kept as luck charms as it was considered bad luck to throw them away.

The Easter Egg was an ancient and universal symbol of life, creation, rebirth and resurrection. Decorating eggs with bright colours and designs predates Christianity and the folk custom of rolling them down hills is in imitation of the movement of the sun across the sky. Before Easter it was usual for children to visit houses in their neighbourhood asking for eggs, which would be hard boiled and used in the Easter games. In later times they asked for money to buy chocolate eggs. If a house owner refused to give anything, the children recited a rhyme putting a hex on their chickens so they laid only stones.

On the Welsh Border on Easter Monday the men carried a chair around the houses decorated with greenery, flowers and ribbons. Each woman in the household sat on this chair and was lifted high into the air. Sometimes the woman's feet were sprinkled with water using a bunch of flowers and the person responsible claimed a kiss as a reward. This ceremony of 'Lifting' was said to celebrate the Resurrection, but it is tempting to be speculative and see it instead as a relic of the former worship of the human representative of the spring goddess in fertility rites practised during this season.

The ancient custom of lifting

April 1st

This is known today as April Fool's Day, a tradition probably going back to the spring carnivals held in classical Rome to celebrate the end of winter when everyone was glad to see the sun and 'played the fool'. When New Year was on March 25th All Fool's Day would have been the end of the festivities to welcome the new year.

In Scotland it is known as Gowk's Day and a gowk was either a cuckoo or a fool. This bird has always been connected with folly and, more importantly, it is the bird whose call heralds the coming of summer. People went out on April Fool's Day 'hunting the gowk' and if they heard its distinctive cry they knew summer was coming. April 1st became a day when it was considered ill-fated to start a new enterprise and if a cuckoo was seen, as well as heard, it was regarded as an omen of death.

April 23rd

St George's Day, and also the alleged birth date and death date of that archetypal Englishman William Shakespeare. In fact George came from Greece and he was not appointed as England's patron saint until the end of the 15th century, even though April 23rd had been a public holiday since 1222. He replaced Edward the Confessor as the English patron saint and his influence seems to have been the result of his popularity among crusaders returning from the Middle East.

The legend of St George says he saved a maiden by killing the dragon that was holding her prison in a cave. This archetypal theme of good conquering evil can be traced back to the Ancient Egyptian myth of Horus and Set and the Hebrew myth of the Archangels Michael and Lumiel (Lucifer). George is said to have been martyred and then, like Christ, he rose from the dead. He seems to be closely associated with the eternal motif of death and rebirth and the battle between good and evil, light and darkness, summer and winter which lies at the heart of the mythic Wheel of the Year and the pagan drama of divine kingship and the sacrificed god.

St George and the Dragon

Because of his important role in the Yuletide mumming plays and the May Day revels, St George has been identified as a Christian version of the old Celtic sun god Bel or Belinus Stewart(1977) notes that the Babylonian deity Bel slew the sea-beast Tiamat just as George killed the nasty old dragon. He also links him with Apollo, Jack-in-the-Green and with the sacred oak tree of Indo-European myth, which was the symbol of the divine king.

Stewart goes on to speculate that St George's role in the Order of the Garter makes him a divine hero who 'guarded and inspired members of a chosen order of sacred kings, or sacrificial victims, whose blood-line was probably inherited from the female side' (1977 p69). Whether this is true or not, Stewart evidently believes that George has an important role connected with St Michael, King Arthur and the Grail Mysteries. It should hardly be needed to remind the reader that the Grail was originally the Cauldron of Inspiration owned by the Welsh witch goddess Ceridwen, who ruled the underworld where the divine hero/sacrificed god descends to, to receive spiritual transformation and rebirth at the hands of the Queen of Hades.

April 30th

This is May Eve or Walpurgis Night when witches, demons, goblins and assorted ghostly creatures travel abroad and attend the witches' sabbath. St Walpurgis or Walburga was an Englishwoman who became the abbess of an 8th century monastery which housed both men and women. Some authorities believe that before she took up the habit she was a Germanic moon goddess, hence her association with May Eve and witches. Covens from all over Europe were said to gather at the Brocken in the Hartz Mountains of

Germany to worship the Horned God. On the summit of the Brocken was the remains of an ancient altar and a sacred spring dating back to prehistoric times.

May Eve was a time for collecting the greenery to be used the next day in the erotic festivities. Superstitious yokels also placed rowan twigs over their barn and cow shed doors to keep the witches and evil spirits away. In his famous diary for April 30th 1870 the Rev. Francis Kilvert of Clyro in Herefordshire notes that he should put out birch twigs over the door to keep the 'old witch' out, although he adds in the great tradition of sexually repressed Victorian clergymen, that young witches are welcome. While I was working on a farm in Somerset in the early Sixties this practice of nailing rowan or birch twigs over doors was still observed. When I remarked upon it the cow man told me it was to stop the local witches 'owl blinking' (cursing) the livestock.

May Garland with doll representing the Goddess Flora

Chapter Four

May Day to Midsummer

Following the early spring festivals of Eostre and the vernal equinox, welcoming the passing of the solstice and the waxing of the sun, summer is greeted by May Day or Beltane on the first of May and is then fully celebrated at Midsummer, June 21st, which is the summer solstice.

May is traditionally the merry month, from the Old German 'murgjaz' or 'mirth'. It is a time for joy and happiness at the coming of the summer and is named after the Greco-Roman goddess Maia, one of the seven sisters of the Pleiades constellation. She was the mother of Mercury or Hermes, the Roman god of wisdom, travel and communication. He is also the planetary ruler of the Zodiac sign Gemini, which ends at the summer solstice.

Maia was sometimes identified with an ancient, pre-classical Italian goddess of the spring called Maia Maistas, the wife of the old fire god Vulcan. She was also known as Fauna, the Mistress of Wild Animals, or as Bona Dea, the Good Goddess. In later Roman times May was dedicated to the flower goddess Flora, hence we have the Latin terms fauna and flora to describe animals and plants.

In the Roman Catholic Church May is said to be the month of the Virgin Mary and during this period she is addressed by the title 'Flower of Hope'. In Celtic times May 1st was Beltane, or 'bright fire' and was the festival of the solar god Bel or Belinus, a Celtic form of Apollo. It was regarded as the first day of summer, just as Samhain on November 1st was the first day of winter.

In the ancient Welsh myths Gwyn ap Nudd, Lord of the Wild Hunt and the underworld, fights for the hand of the daughter of Llud Llaw with Gwythyr ap Creidawl on the first day of May. This is a contest that resembles the tradition of the ritual combat between the Holly King and the Oak King, representing winter and summer. Frazer describes how in pre-classical Italy Rex Nemorensis, the King of the Sacred Grove, was represented by a high priest of the Dianic Mysteries and challenged to ritual combat by a new candidate for the post.

An echo of this ancient tradition survived in the parish of Defynog in Breconshire (Powys), where two boys were elected as the Winter King and the Summer King. These roles were assigned by the goddess Fate in the tossing of a coin. Both wore costumes of birch twigs, but the Winter King had a crown of holly and the Summer King a crown of wild flowers. The two boys walked in procession led by men armed with swords who cleared their way. Another May day custom observed in this parish was for boys to carry a wooden rod around the village boundaries. The bark on this rod had been peeled in a spiral design and it was topped by a painted cockerel.

Towards the end of May comes a Christian and secular festival which also retains memories of the old May Day revels of pagan days. Whitsun, now known as the spring public holiday, was formerly celebrated with feasting and merrymaking, while Oak Apple Day, May 29th, officially celebrated the re-establishment of the monarchy after the Civil War, in fact was a challenge to May Day.

Finally in this period of spring and early summer comes the summer solstice in June, followed by Midsummer's Day. At the solstice the sun enters the Zodiac sign of Cancer the Crab and, while it is high summer, it marks the waning of the sun's power towards the harvest and the autumn. Paradoxically, in our British climate, the best of the summer weather often follows the midsummer period, as early June is often very unsettled.

May 1st

As we have seen, May Eve was spent collecting flowers and greenery for the coming day. The Puritan writer Phillip Stubbes, writing in 1583, complained that young people 'run gadding over night to the woods, groves, hills, and mountains, where they spend all night in pleasant pastimes; and in the morning they return, bringing with them birch and branches of trees to deck their assembles withal... ' He goes on to say that it is reported 'that forty, threescore, or a hundred maids going to the woods over night, there have scarcely the third part of them returned again undefiled.' This may be why it is said to be unlucky to wed during this month. In olden times the tradition of the 'greenwood wedding', or hand fasting, that lasted only for the summer or a year and a day was often made in May.

It was believed to be very lucky if you made the effort to get up and greet the sunrise on May Day morning. At Oxford there is an old custom that the choir of Magdalene College

Raising the Maypole

assemble at dawn on May Day to sing hymns and this is
followed by Morris dancing. This custom is said to date
back to the reign of Henry VIII, but retains the hint of
pagan rites of sun worship at Beltane. Women also rose
early to wash their faces in the morning dew, as this was
said to make blemishes vanish and help you retain your
youth.

On the morning of May Day children went from house to
house carrying small decorated Maypoles or flower

Parading the May Garland - 1800

garlands and they were rewarded with gifts of sweets. This
was a folk memory of the Roman festival in honour of Flora,
when children collected flowers to make images of the
spring goddess and were rewarded for their efforts.

May Day garlands were also made of two circles or hoops of
wood bound with flowers. These were fixed to a pole which
was decorated with more blooms and attached with
coloured ribbons. Sometimes a small female doll,
representing Flora, was also attached to the garland. In

the 1950s Shropshire children fixed a pram wheel to a pole
and covered it with crepe paper and streamers

The most important symbol of the Beltane festivities was
the phallic Maypole. In common with the Christmas Tree,
the Maypole represents the axis mundi or axis cosmos
worshipped by the tribes of Northern Europe. It was the

May Day Revels - 16th Century

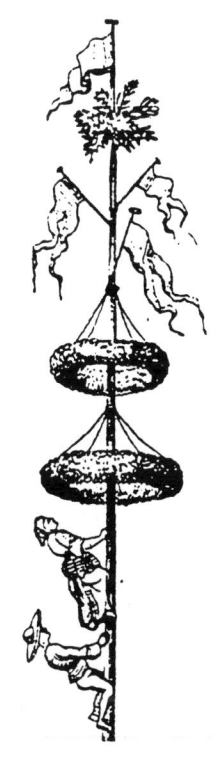

Left: Climbing the Maypole 1870
Right: Tudor Maypole 1500s

World Tree, the Yggdrasil, around which the universe revolved and in Norse mythology it supported the nine worlds of creation in space. In the shamanic tradition it linked the three worlds of the Underworld, Middle Earth and the World of the Gods..

The May Day practice of dancing around the Maypole, and the election of a May King and Queen, dates back to prehistoric times. Rock carvings in Scandinavia for instance depict the 'sacred marriage', or ritual mating, between the human representatives of God and Goddess in the spring to fertilise the land and encourage vegetation growth. This was recognised as late as the 16th century, when a City of London vicar ordered the Maypole to be cut down because it was a symbol of 'idol worship'

In the 17th century, our old friend Phillip Stubbes said of the Maypole ritual:

'their chiefest jewel they bring from thence is their Maypole, which they bring home with great veneration, as thus. They have twenty or forty yoke of oxen, every ox have a sweet nosegay of flowers placed on the tips of his horns, and these oxen draw home this Maypole (this stinking idol, rather), which is covered all over with flowers and herbs, bound round about with strings, from the top to the bottom, and sometimes painted with variable colours, with two or three hundred men, women and children following it with great devotion. And thus being reared up, with hankerchieves and flags hovering on top, they strew the ground round about, bind green boughs about it, set up summer haules, bowers and arbors by it. And then fall they to dance about it, like the heathen people did at the dedication of the idols, whereof this is a perfect pattern, or rather the thing itself.'

The May Day festival was almost eradicated by the Puritans, but this was a process which had been steadily going on for at least a century. Earp (1991), writing about the celebration of May Day in Nottinghamshire, quotes county records from 1541 that refer to payments made to May Day dancers and in 1575 for instance £3 2s 6d was spent 'bringing in the May Day in Nottingham'. However, Earp reports, by 1588 laws were passed making attendance at church on a Sunday a legal obligation. In 1608 eleven men caught watching a football match on a May Day that fell on a Sunday were prosecuted. Morris men who danced on Sunday could also be fined for breaking the Sabbath law.

In some parts of the country a birch or ash was traditionally used for the Maypole, and both these trees have a pagan symbolism. The birch is a tree sacred to the Goddess and represents fertility birth and new beginnings, while the ash is supposed to have been the World Tree of Norse mythology. In Wales the birch was always used for the Maypole and one of the earliest references to 'raising the birch' is in the poetry of a 14th century bard. Maypole raising was closely linked with Morris dancing, or as the Welsh called it, 'summer dancing'. Where garlands were used they were often hung with silver spoons, watches, tankards and symbols of the sun, moon and stars.

In the late 1870s in Herefordshire milkmaids danced around the Maypole with their milk pails on their heads. These pails were decorated with silver spoons and cream jugs which jingled along with the music of the fiddler. Sweeps were also present with their brooms and after the dancing the merry band sat down to a feast of rich fruit cake washed down with rough cider. The May King and Queen sat in a bower while their attendants danced around the Maypole singing patriotic songs.

A Milkmaid from the May Day Revels - 1688

Such Maypole festivals had been revived after the 17th century Civil War. Following the restoration of the Stuart royal dynasty in 1660 for instance, a new Maypole was erected near the church of St Mary-le-Strand in central London. It stood for over fifty years and was a hundred and twenty feet high. In fact it was so heavy that it took twelve sailors using ropes and pulleys to raise it. It was finally taken down in 1717 and used by Sir Isaac Newton as a support for his new telescope.

The May Day celebrations still exist very strongly and Earp (1991) describes the 1980 version which he witnessed in 1980 in the Nottinghamshire village of Wellow. At the pointed end of the village green a stage or platform had

Milkmaids May Day Dance - 1870

been raised and covered with greenery as a bower for the May Queen. On the opposite side of the green was an arch of flowers and evergreens. Led by Morris dancers, the queen and her retinue walked from the village hall, passing through arches of flowers held by small girls. A young boy in front of the procession announced its arrival with a bugle. Once on the platform the May Queen was crowned with a wreath of forget-me-nots by the retiring holder of the

Jolly May Day characters

office and this was followed by Maypole dancing. Afterwards the Morris joined in led by a man carrying a wooden stag's head on a pole. Phillip Stubbes no doubt would have been justly offended by this blatant pagan display that had survived three hundred years after his time.

Robin Hood - outlaw and witch god?

In the 16th century the so-called Robin Hood Games had become a popular feature of May Day. These games featured dancers dressed as Robin Hood, Maid Marian and the Merry Men and they were usually impersonated by the Morris. In Scotland in 1555 these May games became such a threat to the Church that they were banned and their participants punished. Anyone found guilty of taking part was fined 1s 8d and the money was given to the poor. Robin Hood, of course, as well as being a historical outlaw,

King Henry VIII meets 'Robin Hood and his merry men' on May Day

A True Tale of *ROBIN HOOD.*

Or, A Brief Touch of the Life and Death of that renowned Outlaw *Robert* Earl of *Huntington*, vulgarly called *Robin Hood*, who lived and dyed in A. D. 1198. being the 9th. year of the Reign of King *Richard* the First, commonly called *Richard Cœur de Lyon.*

Carefully collected out of the truest Writers of our English Chronicles : And published for the satisfaction of those who desire truth from falshood.

By *Martin Parker.*

Printed for *J. Clark*, *W. Thackeray*, and near *West-Smithfield*, 1687.

Title page of late 17th century book on Robin Hood

on a mythical level was the summer aspect of the witch god and as such is linked with divine figures such as Woden, Herne, Puck and Robin Goodfellow. He is also the Green Man or Jack-in-the-Green, who appears in the Beltane revels as the May King.

The Green Man is the archetypal image of the old pagan Horned God in his role as spirit of vegetation and Lord of the Forest. He takes many forms and aspects of the Green Man can be found in the myths of Cernnunos, Sylvanus, Faunus, Pan, Dionysus, Osiris, Adonis and Baal. The earliest examples of the foliate mask or head of the Green Man peering through a frond of leaves and flowers date from classical times. These early foliate masks were carved on temple walls to represent Dionysus and Sylvanus or Silvanus, the Roman god of the woods. In this context, the

The Woodwose or Wild Man

Green Man symbolises life, death and resurrection as illustrated in the annual cycle of growth and decay in the natural world.

As with the majority of pagan symbols and images, the early Church adopted the Green Man for its own purposes. One of the early examples is to be found carved on the tomb of a saint in 5th century France. In some examples, as in Trier cathedral, foliate heads were removed from pagan temples and placed in churches. However, it was during the Gothic and Romanesque period, coinciding with the building of the great European cathedrals in the Middle Ages, that the foliate mask seems to have become an important feature in Christian art.

The design of the Green Men takes many forms. Sometimes they were a goblin face peering from behind a screen of leaves and flower heads. In other examples plant tendrils or branches extend from the ears, nose or mouth. Other masks have beards and hair made from leaves. In a few cases the whole face or head is in the shape of a single

Early Green Man - from French tomb of saint 4th century CE

83

Jack-in-the-Green 1795

leaf with humanoid features superimposed on it. The tongue sometimes pokes out of the mouth in a blatantly phallic gesture and the mask may have two or three faces, like the Roman god Janus or some Celtic deities.

Later Christian examples show a skull with leaves and plants growing from the eye sockets and jaw. These are supposed to be symbolic images representing the overcoming of death and resurrection on Judgement Day. It is tempting however to see them as an alternative symbol, the skull and phallus representing the twin aspects of the Horned God, as Lord of the Wild Hunt and the Lord of the Wildwood.

Jack-in-the-Green in the streets of Old London Town -
18th century

In the revival of the May Day festivities in the late 18th
and early 19th century the ancient image of the Green Man
was represented by the folklore character known as Jack-
in-the Green, Jack-in-the Hedge or simply Green Jack.

In the 1800s the Jack-in-the-Green became closely
associated with the May Day processions through the
streets of London led by sweeps and milkmaids. They
elected their own Lord and Lady of the May and the Jack
was represented by a pyramid shaped frame of wood or

wickerwork. This was open at the base to allow a man to wear it so that most, if not all, of his body was concealed from view. Green leaves and flowers were then woven into the framework and a slit was left so the person inside could look out and see where he was walking. In some examples Jack sat on a horse and was led at the head of the procession. Where the full regalia was not worn the Jack 0' the Green, as he was often called, just wore a few sprigs of greenery and some flowers in his three cornered hat, and carried a staff decorated with more flowers.

By the end of the 19th century the annual appearances by the Jack-in-the-Greens had faded. This was due not only to the creeping industrialisation of Victorian times, but also their repressive values which frowned upon the drunkenness, permissiveness and sometimes vandalism that accompanied the May Day revels. Legislation passed in 1840 also restricted the use of children as chimney sweeps and this also had an adverse effect on May Day and its celebration.

Traditionally May 1st was a bank holiday, along with Good Friday, Christmas Day and November 1st. In 1871 however Parliament decided that May Day would no longer be a date when the Bank of England closed. In the 1970s, for the wrong reasons, the Labour government restored the holiday, except it was on the first Monday in the month. Throughout the Thatcher years of the 1980s backbench MPs campaigned to ban the holiday, because of its alleged associations with communism and its adoption in the 19th century as a workers' holiday.

In 1993 the Tories announced they would be abolishing it, but after a public outcry led by neo-pagans and Morris dancers it was saved. In 1995 it will be moved for one year only to May 8th to mark the anniversary of VE Day in 1945 and then it will be reinstated, if still on the first Monday of May.

In druidic times two bonfires were lit on May Day and the livestock were driven between them as a protection against disease in the summer months. After the coming of Christianity these Beltane fires were still lit on hills, especially in Wales, Cornwall and Scotland. The special nature of the fire was emphasised by the fact that only selected (sacred) woods could be used to light them. Sometimes the bale fire, as it was called, was lit from nine types of wood and the actual lighting was surrounded by all kinds of taboos.

May Day in south Wales was known as Calan Haf, or 'the first of summer', and the men chosen to light the Beltane fire had to remove all metal objects from their clothing. They then retired to the woods and collected nine different types of kindling for the fire. A circle was cut out in the earth and the sticks were set crossways. It was the tradition that the fire could only be lit by rubbing two oak twigs together until the natural friction created a flame. This procedure has strong pagan elements involving magical observances.

Round cakes of oatmeal were broken up into four pieces and placed inside a bag. Everyone picked a piece and the one who got the last had to jump the fire three times. This gave the selected one good luck and ensured a good harvest. In the old days of course the chosen 'victim' would have been sacrificed for the same purpose. Indeed in the early part of this century there were cases where farmers threw a calf into the flames if there was disease among the herd. Jones (1994) notes that women in the Scottish Highlands

16th century Morris dancers with Maypole

killed a male lamb 'without spot or blemish' for the Beltane sheiling feast, when the flocks were moved to their summer pastures. This feast is shared with friends and neighbours and a toast is drunk to wish for luck, prosperity and the increase of the flocks.

These fires were often lit on May Eve and, as their ancestors had done thousands of years ago, those who watched over them waited to greet the dawn. Sometimes, as the sun rose, the old custom of driving the cattle through the smoke was still observed. In Scotland the young men lit torches from the fire and danced whirling them above their heads to greet 'the new sun' as it rose over the hills.

Offerings of butter, milk and eggs were sometimes left at the site of the Beltane fires or a mixture of eggs and milk was poured on the ground as a libation to the Sidhe or faery folk. In the 18th century, crofters made offerings of whisky and oatmeal to the foxes, crows and eagles, asking them to spare the flocks. In Perthshire, as in south Wales, young boys cooked oat cakes on the Beltane fire and selected pieces until a 'chosen one' was found. He was said to be 'the sacrifice to Bel'. This tradition was common in the Highlands until at least the 1890s. After the fires burnt down the ashes were collected and scattered on the field as a fertility charm.

One of the most famous surviving customs of May Day is the Old 'Oss of Padstow in Cornwall. The Old Oss, or Red Oss, which in its present form dates from 1932, consists of a circular frame or hoop about five or six feet in diameter, which is carried on the shoulders of the operator. This frame is covered in a black cloth that reaches down to his knees. A tall pointed 'cap', like a wizard's headgear, covers the head, with a face mask that has a red lolling tongue, white circles around the eyes, grey whiskers or 'beard' and a horse's plume. There is also a Blue Oss, dating from the 1900s, and it sets off from a different place and takes a separate route through the town. It has been suggested they represent a winter and summer horse.

The festival of the Old Hoss begins at midnight on May Eve, when the houses are decorated with greenery and a Maypole is set up. As the church clock strikes midnight the town is serenaded with the famous Night Song. In the old days boys collected money and threw buckets of water over anyone who was not wearing a sprig of greenery. The next morning the two horses set off around the town with the Teaser or Dancer leading, waving his club and teasing the beast. Sometimes the Oss dashes into the crowd and catches a young woman. She is said to be very lucky and this looks like an old fertility ritual being re-enacted in modern times. The procession collects money for charity and sings the May Song, a verse of which refers to St George, and also to a folk character called Auntie Ursula Birdwood, who may be a memory of the summer goddess. After a large lunch at the Golden Lion, both horses meet up and dance under the Maypole.

Another Beltane hobby horse is at Minehead in Somerset and again this ceremony begins on May Eve, and significantly at a crossroads at dawn, or the ceremony cannot go ahead. The Horse consists of a large frame seven or eight feet long and pointed at both ends like a boat. It is covered by canvas painted with circles and the words 'sailor's Horse'. It is decorated on the top with ribbons and strips of cloth to resemble a mane. Originally the Minehead Horse had a cow's tail, now a rope, and a wooden head covered with hare skin and with snapping jaws.

The Horse is accompanied by fishermen dressed up as sailors and an accordionist. They process through the streets, playing and singing a traditional song and in the last century were joined by a group of men known as Gullivers, who wore pointed caps decorated with ribbons and face masks. They collected money from houses, but local legend says the practice stopped in the 1900s when one of the group killed a policeman in a fight. No public record of this event can be found however.

May 8th

This is the date of the famous Furry or Floral Dance in Helston, Cornwall. It is also the feast day of St Michael, the archangel who fought and defeated Lucifer in the Battle of Heaven, casting him down to Earth where he must remain as Lord of the World until he, and humanity, are redeemed. St Michael is the patron saint of Helston and many churches in the West Country are dedicated to him. These were early Celtic churches built on pagan sites and in the 8th century they were re-dedicated to Michael in his role as the guardian of the gates of Hell and vanquisher of the powers of darkness.

The local Michael legend states that the battle between the archangel and the Devil took place at Mont St Michel in Brittany. At the height of the battle Michael was forced to flee and he sought sanctuary on what is now St Michael's Mount in Cornwall, a former site of druidic worship. As the Devil could not cross the sea, he hurled a large stone that sealed the gates of Hell across the Channel. Unfortunately the missile fell short of its intended target and crashed into the village of Helston, where it can still be seen in the wall of the Angel Hotel. Nobody was hurt because the village was under the protection of St Michael and for this reason they decided to celebrate his feast day every year.

That is the Christian version but it is pretty obvious the Floral Dance is much older. It begins on May 1st when the band parades through the streets in the morning playing the famous Floral Dance tune and accompanied by crowds of children. Seven days later the festival proper begins with a special service in St Michael's church followed by dancing in the streets. The first dance is led by young people dressed up as St Michael, St George, the Dragon, Robin Hood and his Merry Men etc. The adult dance follows at noon with the men in top hats and morning dress and the women in their best summer frocks. They dance along the streets and in and out of the shops and houses 'for luck'. After a civic lunch, the final dance in the evening is led again by the young people and everyone joins in.

May 13th

This is Old May Day and at Abbotsbury in Dorset was celebrated as Garland Day. The children collected wild flowers from the woods and hedgerows and wove them into May garlands that were then hung from poles. These were paraded through the village 'for luck' and the children were awarded for their efforts with silver coins. At the conclusion of the procession all the monies collected were shared among the children and the garlands were laid around the War Memorial. When Abbotsbury was a fishing village the children took their garlands to the beach and fishing boats took them out to sea, where they were scattered on the waves.

Whitsun

Some of the pagan celebrations marking the start of the summer appear to have survived in this Christian festival towards the end of May, which is now called the spring bank holiday. Herefordshire villagers in the 19th century used to decorate the church with leaves and birch twigs on Whit Sunday or greenery from a yew tree. In ancient times the yew was regarded as a tree of eternal life and resurrection, and groves of yews around old churches may predate Christian uses of the site.

Collections were made locally to buy the traditional Whitsun ale and the celebration of this festival in the 17th century included dances, bowling and archery displays. A Whitsun King and Queen were selected to preside over the games and they went around the village or town giving out the famous Banbury cakes from a basket. Often the Lord and Lady, as they were called, were accompanied by Morris dancers, a painted hobby horse and a stuffed owl. The latter was hung up in a long shed decorated with greenery and called the King and Queen's Bower.

On Whit Monday in Kingsteignton in Devon the famous Ram Fair was held. The carcass of a young ram was carried through the town decorated with ribbons and flowers. It was later roasted and distributed to all the town's folk. This custom is said to have started when a stream supplying water to the town dried up. The local priest told his flock to pray to God and like a miracle a new spring burst forth from a nearby meadow. In thanks that their prayers were answered the people killed and ate a ram. This sounds like a folk memory of sacrificial offerings to a geni loci associated with a local sacred spring.

May 29th

The Maypole and May Day were banned during the reign of the Puritan tyrant Oliver Cromwell and his fun-hating gang of religious bigots. In fact constables and churchwardens were told to remove by force any Maypole that was erected by the people. With the return of Charles Stuart as King Charles II on May 29th, 1660 this date became an important one in the folklore calendar, although it is almost forgotten now. In fact it often overshadowed May Day and much of the latter's symbolism was briefly transferred to it.

Oak Apple Day was for many years a public holiday and it was traditional to wear an oak leaf on the day. Anyone who did not, or refused to do so when challenged, was in danger of physical violence. In some parts of the country it was called Oak & Nettle Day, because anyone who refused to wear the oak leaf and recognise the king was painfully beaten with nettles. The image of King Charles hiding in the oak trees to escape his enemies became an acceptable version of the Green Man or Jack-in-the-Green and was featured as a popular inn sign.

Herefordshire people danced through the streets waving oak boughs and wearing flowers in their hats or hair. Young men dared each other to climb church steeples and place an oak bough on its tip. Horses had their harnesses covered in oak leaves and up to 1900 even railway engines were garlanded with flowers and oak branches. The wearing of the oak leaf to remember King Charles seems to have survived into the 20th century and only died out with the start of the last war.

June 21st/22nd

This is the summer solstice, widely celebrated in northern Europe and also, judging from the survival of midsummer customs in Cornwall, Scotland and Wales, in Celtic countries. The church took over the solstice as St John's Day (June 24th) and this soon became known as Midsummer's Day.

Since the early 1900s the main public event associated with the summer solstice has been the annual ceremony held by a modern Order of Druids at Stonehenge to greet the sunrise. The henge was first associated with druidic worship in the 17th century, even though there is no firm evidence to suggest the druids had anything to do with the circle.

The druidic revivalists of the 18th and 19th centuries were a motley bunch of Freemasons, antiquarians, religious fanatics and even British Israelites, who believed the Celts were one of the lost tribes of the Babel. The 'druidism' they created, which survives today, had little connection with the ancient Celtic religion, drawing its creative inspiration from the Old Testament and a supposed pagan cultus of sun worship followed by the Celts.

In the 1970s and 1980s a Stonehenge Free Festival was established at the site. At its height it attracted 35,000 worshippers of sex, drugs and rock n' roll, but in 1985 the newly formed quango English Heritage, set up by the Tories to exploit the commercial potential of ancient monuments, joined forces in an unholy alliance with the National Trust, local landowners, the MOD and the police to have the festival, and the druidic ceremony, banned.

Today those seeking sex, drugs etc find what they are looking for at the Glastonbury Festival at nearby Pilton, while those wishing to welcome the sunrise at Stonehenge are forced to brave razor wire, guard dogs and riot police.

June 23rd

Divination featured strongly in the folklore of St John's Eve. It was when young women seeking life partners sought supernatural advice. Female servants in Wales went to the nearest holy well at midnight to wash an intimate item of clothing. They did this in the belief that as they were washing an apparition of their future lover or husband would appear.

Often, by prior arrangement, the master of the house kept the rendezvous and, if he was a widower, then shortly afterwards she might become a bride.

Midsummer Eve was chosen for divination because it was one of the three 'spirit nights' of the year when faeries, witches and ghosts walked abroad and could be seen by anyone, not just the psychic. The other two nights were May Eve and Hallowe'en. Sprigs of St John's Wort were placed over the doors of houses on this night to protect the occupants from evil influences. If the plant was gathered at midnight on Midsummer's Eve, especially if it was also a full moon, it was said to possess magical powers of healing. A sprig placed under the pillow brought dreams of a future lover and sleep untroubled by nightmares.

On Midsummer's Eve in Scotland lovers met at the standing stones of Stennir on Orkney to drink water from a nearby spring. They then went to the Stone of Odin, which has a hole in it about five feet from the ground. The custom was to link hands through the hole and make vows of faithfulness and undying love. Old people told stories of mysterious lights and the flames of fire being seen in the circle which vanished if anyone approached.

June 24th

The lighting of midsummer bonfires in the Celtic countries of the British Isles and in Northern Europe was widespread. The solstice was also marked by torchlit processions, the lighting of tar barrels and the rolling of blazing cartwheels down streets or hillsides.

In Orkney the material for the fires were peat, faggots and heather, which had been collected by the children weeks in advance. Before each fire was lit an animal bone was tossed onto the pyre - hence the term bon-fire or bone fire. This act was said to commemorate a Christian martyr, but was more likely the relic of animal sacrifices.

As at Beltane, the livestock were driven through the smoke of the bonfires to purify them of disease. To add extra power to the rite, the farmer and his lads lit torches from the fire and circumrabulated each of the fields clockwise. Torches were also used to fumigate the byres where the cattle were who were pregnant, to prevent stillbirths and ensure only healthy calves were born.

Until the 19th century in Cornwall midsummer bonfires were lit on every hill across the county. In Penzance young men balanced blazing barrels on poles, while firecrackers were let off and torches brandished in the air. In 1800 it is recorded that a farmer killed his best cow and threw it in the flames and echoes of human sacrifices can be found at St Cleer, where a witches hat, besom and oak-handled sickle were offered to the flames. As Straffon (1993) remarks, a pagan festival has become, under the influence of Christianity the burning of witches, who were themselves pagan survivalists.

Recently the midsummer bonfires have been revived by the Federation of Old Cornwall Societies. However it seems the pagan glories of the past have faded away and today the highlight of the ceremonies is the singing of hymns and a pastie. In Northumberland, by way of contrast, the Old Ways are kept alive with a huge bonfire on July 4th (Old Midsummer's Eve) in a tradition that has continued for over two hundred years. In Wales the so-called 'summer branch' was made and paraded at the solstice. This was a birch pole with ribbons, a wreath of wild flowers and a gilded weather-cock, symbol of the sun and fertility, on its top. It was traditional to guard the branch through the night from attacks mounted by rival villages. It was thought very unlucky if a village lost its branch and had to watch it paraded through another one. These branches were the focal point of summer dances that began on St John's Day and continued until the end of the month.

July 25th

On this day the Horn Fair takes place in Sussex and it is also the feast day of St James. Originally the horns were worn on the head of one of the revellers. At the similar Charlton Horn Fair in Kent, which was first recorded in the 16th century, everyone present wore horns and ate ram's horns made of sugar and gingerbread.

In the Sussex version a whole sheep was roasted and eaten after a cricket match between rival villages. The batsman who scored the most runs was awarded with a sheep's skull with horns. This is believed to bring luck and fertility and if he is single then it is said he will soon be married. Valiente (1962) quotes this festival as an example of the survival of the worship of the Horned God.

Dancing round the Maypole - a typical rural scene

Chapter Five

Lammas to Harvest Home

Lammas (August 1st) to the autumn equinox at the end of September marked the period in the agricultural cycle devoted to harvesting and the safe gathering in of the crop. Obviously the harvest gathering differed from place to place depending on the climate and it might be gathered earlier in Scotland for instance. The word Lammas comes from the Saxon 'halfmaesse' or 'loaf mass' and it refers to the Mass celebrated with the first wheat or corn from the harvest. It is the 'first offering' to God of the fruits of the harvest.

In Celtic times the beginning of August was known as Lughnasadh and dedicated to the god Lugh. His festival was celebrated with pre-harvest games, horse races, marriages and general merrymaking. Before the August bank holiday was moved to the end of the month it was still a time in the countryside for fairs and horse racing. In post-industrial times it was the beginning of the Wakes, or compulsory factory shutdowns, in the North Country. This tradition still survives - even among Japanese companies in Wales!

Lugh was, and indeed is for the Old Gods never die, an Irish Celtic god 'with many skills' in arts and crafts. Lughnasadh was founded by the god to honour his foster-

Harvest wagon in 19th century Gloucestershire - an
imitation of the procession of the image of the Norse
fertility god Frey in his wagon at the harvest festival in
late August in pagan Scandanavia

mother, the earth goddess Taitu. In Gaul (France) he was known as Lugus and had a role similar to the winged messenger of the Gods, Mercury. The Romans, as with all the Celtic deities they encountered, regarded Lugh or Lugus as one of their pantheon and they compared him with Mercury as well. Some authorities however claim that his cultus represented that of the solar god Apollo.

The purpose of the Lammas rites was to prepare for the harvest and perform ceremonies that would promote a good one and fine weather to bring it in. It often featured love making in the fields to encourage the crops to ripen and in classical times sacrifices to the corn goddesses Ceres and Demeter. In the 12th century Gerald of Wales described the Christianised version of the Lughnasadh rituals, when men and women 'danced in a frenzy' around the churchyard. As they danced they mimed with their hands and feet the arts and crafts of their employment, such as cobbling, ploughing, smithcraft, weaving and sewing.

In both Scotland and Ireland the Lammas festival was a time for handfasting or marriages that only lasted a year and a day. Rural fairs were used to meet partners and perform the handfasting. The next year the couples met at the fair, either to renew their vows or break up the relationship. As can be expected, such blatant pagan practices were censured by the Church, who eventually banned them. However they continued in secret, without the priest's knowledge or the parents' permission.

As it was the Church took over Lughnasadh with its halfmaesse and the tradition of the Lammas corn. On the Sunday nearest to August 1st the new corn from the harvest, if gathered, was brought into the church and blessed by the priest. Sometimes the full Mass was given or alternatively the new corn was placed on the altar while the congregation offered up a prayer of thanksgiving, praying also for good weather to complete the harvest. In the Middle Ages the priest, who was also a clerk, often presided over the payment of half-yearly rents due on Lammas, which was one of the four quarter days of the agricultural year.

As late as the 1840s in Scotland the midsummer fires were transferred from mid-June to Lammas. The fires were lit on the last day of July, Lammas Eve or St Margaret's day. A huge cartwheel was heated in the fire until its metal rim glowed red hot. This was then rolled down a hillside and its passage was eagerly watched to divine omens for the harvest. This fiery wheel represents the sun as it descends from the height of the sky at midsummer, down into the underworld of the winter months.

August 10th

On the Wednesday after this date the custom of well dressing was carried out in Derbyshire. This custom goes back to Celtic and pre-Celtic ceremonies to honour the geni loci or spirits of the well and the gods and goddesses of water with offerings of flowers and dancing. The Celtic Church took over the holy wells during the 5th and 6th centuries and re-dedicated them to their saints, who often shared myths and symbols with pagan deities, or to the Virgin Mary, the Christianised version of the Great Mother Goddess.

In Derbyshire traditions of well dressing go back to the 1300s at least and it is said the practice originated in thanksgiving for deliverance from the plague, flood or drought. At first the wells were decorated with simple garlands of flowers, but in the 1800s the procedure became more complicated with elaborate mosaics made from leaves, berries, pressed flowers, bark and moss pressed on to a clay covered board to create pictures. Pebbles, shells, sand, and other natural materials were added, but glass, metal, plastic or any other human-made material was strictly taboo. Today the pictures usually have a local or Christian reference.

In the second weeks of August the Burryman's Parade takes place at South Queensferry on the Firth of Forth in Scotland. The actual Burryman is a well-built man swathed in white flannel from head to foot, so he resembles the famous Michelin Man in the old tyre adverts. This outer covering is then covered in thistle burrs until nothing can be seen of the cloth. A pair of eye holes are left and a gap for the mouth so the man inside can breath. He wears a head-dress of wild roses and carries two staves decorated with flowers.

At about nine o'clock in the morning of the annual Ferry Fair, the Burryman and his attendants set out to walk around the town. This is done so slowly that the journey is often not completed until the late afternoon. At each house money is given to the Burryman and this is spent at the Fair. It is considered very lucky to see the Burryman, and very unlucky if you do not give him money.

Today the ceremony is said to commemorate the arrival of Queen Margaret in Scotland at Ferry harbour in the 11th century, but the Burryman seems to be a relic of a far distant past. Hole (1976) speculates that he is a pre-Christian figure connected with the harvest, while McNeill (1968 Vol 4), noting his resemblance to the Leaf Man of central Europe and Green Jack, suggests he may be a scapegoat who took away the evil from the community and was sacrificed for its good.

The Puck Fair

A strange ritual is carried out around the 11th or 12th of August (Old Lammas Day) at Killorgin, Co. Kerry in Ireland, which may be a folk memory of the worship of the Horned God. For three days the market square is dominated by a thirty foot high platform and high on this scaffolding stands a magnificent billy goat. He is usually a wild goat who is specially caught from the surrounding countryside and has the honour, whether he appreciates it or not, of presiding over the Puck Fair.

On the first day of the fair, known as Gathering Day, the goat is paraded through the streets on the back of a lorry led by a pipe band. The Puck, as the goat is called, is attended by boys dressed in green and has flower wreaths draped around its neck. A little girl, who is the queen of the fair, crowns the goat with a tinsel crown. The animal is then lashed to the platform and raised into position on the scaffolding, to the cry "The Puck King of Ireland". During its captivity the goat is fed the best food and is released into the wild on the last day of the fair, known as Scattering Day.

The local legend says that the event commemorates a famous goat who came down from the hills and warned the village about the coming of Cromwell's troops in the 17th century. Murray (1931) however sees this ancient ceremony of the Puck King as a survival of the worship of the incarnate Horned God, and the sacrifice of the divine king who was replaced by an animal substitute. She believes that in its original form this ceremony may date back to the Neolithic period.

August 24th

On the Saturday nearest to this date, which is St Bartholomew's Day, a strange folk ritual with a possible pagan origin is observed in the village of West Witton, Yorkshire.

It is known as the Burning of the Bartle and take place during a three day festival known as the Witton Feast. It is said to commemorate the hunting down of a sheep rustler sometime in the 16th century allegedly on St Bart's Day. This thief was called Bartle, after the saint, and was chased by monks to the slopes of nearby Penhill, where he was killed.

Taylor (1987) described the ceremony as he saw it in 1985. First of all the police sealed off the village and at 9 p.m. a procession of about a hundred and fifty people gathered. At their head was the image of the Bartle carried on the shoulders of one of the men. This effigy looked like a scarecrow, with a cap, white beard and eyes lit by battery operated light bulbs that blinked on and off.

This procession moved along the village streets, stopping at public houses and the cottages of the elderly and sick. At each stop a special rhyme was sung listing local landmarks and the fate of the original Bartle as he tore his clothes, broke his knee and then his neck and finally met his end. At the houses of the bed-ridden and elderly the Bartle was 'shown' and presented to the people who were at the windows on the first floor. Taylor was told by the Chanter, who led the procession, that this presentation to the old and sick was "a serious business".

The Chanter who oversees the Burning of the Bartle and the attendants come from two local families who have participated in the ritual for generations. In earlier days the Bartle was paraded on a cart pulled by six of the strongest men from the families. They were also responsible for making the effigy and this was always surrounded by secrecy. The mask was removed each year before the Bartle was burnt and re-used for the next year.

Taylor's researches into local folklore unearthed the story of the Penhill Giant. Once upon a time a giant lived on Penhill and called himself the son of Thor, the Norse thunder and weather god. He terrorised the locality and everyone was terrified of his wrath. Each day the giant's pet boar hound, Wolfshead, drove a herd of pigs up the hill and the giant stood at the age of his fortress and counted them.

One day, while out walking, the giant saw a flock of sheep and ordered his dog to attack them. This the beast did and soon many sheep lay dead or dying. As this slaughter was going on the shepherd called Gunda came on the scene and begged the giant to call off the hound. The giant was highly amused but, seeing she was very beautiful, he decided to rape her. Gunda however bravely fought off the giant's advances and ran away. The giant ordered his hound to chase and catch her, but she hit the dog on the nose with a large stone and it slunk away whimpering in pain. Enraged the cruel giant smashed her to the ground with his club.

A few days later, as the giant was counting the pigs driven up from the valley by his dog, he noticed a boar was missing. The angry giant beat Wolfshead and ordered him to go out and find the missing animal. When the giant heard his dog howling he went to the spot and found the boar dead with an arrow in its heart. The giant called all the local archers to the hill and demanded to know which one had carried out the dastardly deed. In the meantime Wolfshead, fed up with his master's temper and beatings, had run away and the giant tracked him down and shot him with an arrow.

None of the archers would admit to the killing of the pig and the frustrated giant ordered all the fathers to bring their youngest sons to the top of Penhill by the next sunset and if the pig slayer did not confess he would kill them all. A hermit then stepped from the crowd and said that as the next day was Thor's Day (Thursday) if a drop of any of the children's blood was spilt the giant would not see his castle, dead or alive. Despite this warning, the fathers brought their sons to the hill, but the hermit appeared again and told them not to worry as no harm would come to them.

As the crowd assembled, the giant's steward came to him and said he had experienced a disturbing dream in which ravens, omens of death and the familiar spirits of Odin, had been flying over the castle. The giant was angry at this and he hit the steward over the head with his club, leaving him for dead. Despite his injuries the man managed to gather together nine armfuls of fish, nine bales of straw and nine bags of peat and he set these alight in the great hall of the giant's castle.

The giant meanwhile had begun to walk down the hill towards the crowd. He had only walked a short distance when he found nine of his pigs dead on the path in front of him. After taking nine more strides he saw nine more, and after three strides yet another nine. By the time he reached the crowd he was speechless with rage. Then the giant looked back over his shoulder and saw that his castle was ablaze. Then from the mist the shades of Gunda and Wolfshead materialised. Filled with dread and horror the giant backed away towards the cliff edge. As the crowd watched in terror, Gunda released the hell hound and it leapt for the giant's throat. Locked in mortal combat both the dog and its ex-master fell over the cliff and were never seen again.

Taylor's interpretation of this strange legend, and the Burning of the Bartle, is that it is associated with an ancient pagan ritual. He also believes there was once a hill figure carved on Penhill similar to the Cerne Abbas giant, and he claims to have found a pattern of landscape alignments linking the hill with other ancient sites nearby. The actual giant Taylor identifies with the Norse fertility god Frey, whose sacred animal was a boar and whose harvest festival was celebrated at the end of August. Wolfshead is either one of Odin's guardians or the Fenris Wolf, symbol of the powers of chaos and darkness in the universe. Taylor further links the giant with Bel, Robin Hood and the Green Man. Hole (1976) sees the Bartle figure as either the spirit (god) of the nearby Middleham forest or an ancient deity of the harvest.

It is interesting that the Bartle is said to resemble a scarecrow for this is an image associated with the sacrificial victim or divine king sacrificed to fertilise the land and bring a good harvest. The scarecrow was sometimes called the Jack-of-Lent and this referred to the popular custom of stoning or hitting with sticks a social outcast during Lent.

Folk names for the scarecrow included 'bogey', meaning an evil ghost or goblin, and 'mawkin', meaning a spirit of the dead. Scarecrows were originally used as magical images to protect the crops from harm and also took on the role of the substitute for the sacrificial victim.

September 4th

The first Monday, after the first Sunday, after September 4th, was traditionally the day for the performance of the

The Scarecrow - ancient rural symbol of the geni terra, or spirit of the land, the Sacrificed God and the Divine King

Abbots Bromley Horn Dance. The Horn Dance is performed on the edge of the ancient Needwood Forest, between Burton-on-Trent and Stafford. The first written record of the Dance dates from 1686 and a note made in the margin of this record states that the writer saw it performed as a young man and 'the custom was continued until the warre.' (English Civil War). Shipman (1982) says the Dance was first performed at the three day fair to celebrate St Bart's Day (August 24th) in 1226. It moved to its present date because of the change in the calendar in 1752.

However, the 17th century account says that the Dance was originally performed around Christmas, New Year and Twelfth Night, but was then transferred to St Bart's Day or after Wake's Sunday in early September. There is also a tradition that it used to be celebrated in the summer months after church service to raise money for the poor. The original date around the turning of the year would seem to be appropriate as the Dance features men dressed as animals and we know that such rites were performed at that time, possibly representing the Wild Hunt.

The performance is organised by two local families and features six men carrying reindeer antlers mounted on poles. They were originally painted white and red, three each, until 1952 when they changed to white and blue. In the 1970s they were white with brown tips and dark brown with gold tips. In the late 17th century these horns were kept in the town hall, but now they reside in the church and are guarded by the vicar. In addition to the six principal dancers there is also a she-male dressed as Maid Marian, a hobby horse, a jester or Fool, a boy carrying a bow and arrow, another with a triangle and a musician who plays a fiddle or accordion.

Originally the dancers wore their own clothes with white and blue ribbons attached and their faces blacked up like guisers. Then in 1887 the vicar's daughters designed and made a special costume of green tunics, brown trousers tucked into stockings and beret-like caps. Thus dressed the dancers collect the antlers from the church, dedicated to St Nicholas, and after a blessing from the vicar set off for twelve hours of dancing around the parish boundaries. Their appearance at houses and farms is regarded as a sign of good luck. The dance is timed so it arrives at the manor house for lunch and it ends in the late evening after a tour of local pubs.

The local story is that the Dance springs from celebrations when the villagers were granted hunting rights by the lord of the manor in the 12th century. Most folklorists seem to agree that the Horn Dance began in medieval times, although some say it was a development of the Morris. Alford (1978) suggests the antlers were a gift from the lord of the manor to add grandeur to the appointment of the dancers. Shipman (1982) looks northward to the Saxons and Danes who settled in area.

There is an old tradition that the antlers must never leave the parish, and when performances were held in London a replica set had to be taken. Since the members of the Horn Dance are sometimes not visitors to the church this has caused some problems in the past with dissent between the vicar and his parishioners. In recent years the event has attracted a large number of neo-pagans and witches and the vicar has been somewhat uneasy at their presence in the church at the beginning of the ceremony. Rumours indicate that the last vicar, who was an evangelical, left the parish after an incident during a baptism when he allegedly ordered the mother of a baby to leave because she was possessed by the Devil. He is said to have refused to baptise the baby because it was 'a child of Satan'.

September 21st/22nd & 29th

The autumn equinox, when night and day are equal, falls around September 21st, when the sun enters the earthy sign of Virgo the Virgin, the corn maiden or goddess. The equinox was Christianised as Michaelmas or the Feast of St Michael of All Angels on September 29th, one of the old quarter days.

Michaelmas was the time for hiring fairs, when farmers took on new labourers or the Mop Fairs were, as the name suggests, female domestics were hired or renewed their existing contracts for another year. In Scotland memories of sacrificial rites survived in a special meal of lamb and Michael's Cake made from grain from every crop grown that year. This was followed by horse racing along the beach and dancing until the early hours. Such feasts were celebrated by the Welsh nearer to Lammastide and involved the building of the so-called Lammas Houses. These were huts made of branches with earth for a roof and they were used for the special feast of milk, apples, cheese, apple pies and cream to celebrate the harvest. Afterwards they were set on fire.

Harvest End

The gathering in of the harvest was a time for folk rituals to appropriate the corn spirit and Mother Earth. In Scotland the Cailleach, Hag or Auld Wife makes another appearance as the name for the last sheaf gathered in by

Taking home the last sheaf - Cornwall 1890s

the harvesters. In some areas it was known as the Bride or Corn Maiden, corresponding to the spring goddess Brigid who has matured into the earth mother of the summer. In other places it was the Kern Baby and is the spirit of the corn, born from the Great Rite between the God and Goddess at Beltane.

Whatever it was called the cutting and gathering of the last sheaf in the last field was surrounded by magic and taboo. In the Scottish examples, the person who cut down the Cailleach regarded it as a great honour bringing luck for the year ahead. On the Isle of Islay the sheaf was cut and dressed as a corn dolly complete with a dress. She was then

The last sheaf - Somerset 19th century

hung on the farmhouse wall until the next year's ploughing, when she was taken down, broken up and scattered by the women in the fields or fed to the horse pulling the plough.

In north Pembrokeshire in west Wales a similar doll was made, called the Hen Wrach or Old Hag. The farm labourers took turns to throw their sickles at the last sheaf until it was cut down. The successful one was rewarded with a jug of ale and the hag was taken to the farmhouse by the ploughman, who had to do the deed without being seen or getting it wet. If he failed, he was stripped naked and had buckets of water thrown over him. If he managed the act he was given a jug of beer and the Hag was hung in the hall until the next harvest.

The cutting of the Corn Maiden was also regarded as lucky and the sheaf was fashioned into the shape of a young woman and dressed in a white frock with ribbons. Sometimes the last sheaf was called the Maidenhead or simply the Head. In Aberdeenshire the Maiden was fed to the first colt born in the new year. If the farmer's wife neglected to do this it was said the animal would sicken and die and the harvest would be a poor one. An alternative custom was to feed the sheaf to the oldest cow on Christmas morning.

On English farms the ceremony of Crying the Neck was carried out. All the reapers threw their sickles at the last sheaf because, unlike in Scotland and Wales, it was considered unlucky to be the man responsible for the deed. It was therefore left as a game of chance. If the man who cut it was identified he was jostled and had corn stalks thrown at him. In early times he would have been ritually killed so his blood poured into the earth.

Once the Neck had been cut, it was lifted up into the air by the Harvest Lord, if one was elected, or the oldest farm worker to the cry "I have it, I have it!", to which the other men replied "What have ee?" and he responded: "The Neck, the Neck. I have the Neck!". Then one of the young lads would snatch the Neck from the older man and run with it in triumph to the farmhouse.

In Herefordshire and on the Welsh Border the last sheaf was actually tied up to represent the four legs and body of a mare. The workers then threw their sickles at the sheaf to cut off the ears of corn. Whoever succeeded had the honour of sitting opposite the master at the Harvest Supper. One

Traditional Scandanavian Corn Dolly

strange Welsh custom that links harvest with Hallowe'en was the Bwca Llwyd or Grey Bogey. This was recorded in 1919 by a folklorist who told the director of the National Museum of Wales. Apparently the canvas used during harvest time to carry the corn was transformed into the Bwca by packing straw into one corner to make a head. This was then fixed with harvest gloves as ears and buttons as eyes. A pitchfork was used to hold it up while a man hid under the canvas. This was then taken around the villages and nearby farms to frighten people at night.

Harvest Home

Following the gathering in of the last sheaf came Harvest Home, which was celebrated with the Harvest Supper laid on by the farmer for his workers. In rural parts of England the corn dolly was brought home in a harvest wain that was decorated with flowers and boughs of oak and ash. This wagon was drawn by four or six carthorses garlanded with flowers and with gleaming horse brasses on their collars. The reapers sat on top of the wagon blowing horns and singing bawdy songs, while the other workers walked behind. Sometimes the waggoner wore a woman's dress.

The Harvest Supper was always a huge feast with roast beef, chickens, plum pudding, ginger cake, cider and ale, cheese and hare. In Herefordshire the main meat was goose, the traditional feast for Michaelmas and the sacred bird of the goddess of winter, Holda. In 18th century Cardiganshire the supper consisted of mutton and potatoes washed down with gallons of beer. In the 19th century beef, onions and peas were followed by milk pudding. This followed a harvest tea served in the fields of bread, cheese, jam, fruit cake and gooseberry pie.

In Scotland the Harvest Supper was known as the Feast of the Maiden. The man who cut down the last sheaf was given the honoured seat next to the master as Lord of the Harvest. The young woman who had plaited the corn dolly took her place alongside him as the Lady. She was treated with the greatest respect and the man was regarded as her consort, not the other way round. The meal itself consisted of haggis, roast chicken, cheese, herb dumplings, oat cakes and plum pudding, washed down with jugs of beer and tankards of whisky.

After the eating and drinking there was dancing to the bagpipes or a fiddle and the corn dolly was paraded in front of the assembly to loud cheers. It was toasted and the workers shouted "Here's to the one who helped us with the harvest!". The dancing went on until dawn when the tired farm workers finally made their weary way home, still singing and dancing as they went.

With increased mechanisation, the old customs of Harvest End and Harvest Home gradually ceased in the countryside. It was largely replaced by the more sedate Harvest Festival in church, created by the eccentric Cornish vicar, Rev R.S.Hawker, in 1843. This was a Christian version of the offering of firstfruits transferred from Lammas to the autumn equinox. It is still a popular service, with the church decorated with vegetables, bread and fruit, which is afterwards distributed to old people's homes. Even the odd corn dolly appears in church at this service and is a reminder of the fertility rites once performed at harvest-time in honour of the Earth Mother.

Chapter Six

Hallowe'en

Samhain (November 1st) was one of the most important dates in the ancient Celtic calendar and this is reflected today in the popularity of the time as a folk festival. The Celts divided their year into only two seasons - summer and winter. Winter began on November 1st, while summer commenced on Beltane or May Day. In Northern Europe a similar custom was followed, with winter beginning at the October full moon and summer at the full moon in April. Both the Celts and the Northern tribes based their calendars on the lunar cycle, counting by nights and not days, and recognising a thirteen month year.

In Wales Samhain Eve or Hallowe'en was known as Nos Calen Coef or 'the eve of the winter's calend (first)' and it marked the end of the summer. Sometimes Harvest Home was delayed until as late as this and was called ffest y grawch or 'the Hag's feast', referring to the Crone or Hag Goddess who rules from Samhain to Candlemas. Until the end of the 19th century many farmers slaughtered pigs and surplus cattle at this time and salted the meat for the winter. This dates back to Celtic times and before. Any meat left over from the salting was given to the local poor.

Samhain was the festival of the dead in pagan times and was Christianised as the Feast of All Saints. In the early Church this was celebrated on February 21st or May 1st or 13th. In the 9th century the Pope decided to transfer it to Samhain and he made November 2nd All Soul's Day, when prayers were to be offered to the souls of the departed and those who were waiting in Purgatory for entry into Heaven. Today both Christian and pagan beliefs are mixed up in the Hallowe'en period, which extends from October 31st to November 5th.

Punkie Night

The last Thursday in October is called Punkie Night in Somerset and it features children carrying 'punkies' or lanterns made from hollowed out mangelwurzels with candles inside. These are carried by strings threaded through holes in the top of the lanterns by the children, who visit houses begging for money. It is considered to be unlucky not to give to the punkie carriers.

Hole (1978) reports that a new constable tried to put a stop to the custom before the last war. A complaint was made to the Chief Constable of Somerset and the ban was quickly lifted. Nobody locally seems to know when or why the custom began, but it is generally assumed by most folklorists that it is connected with Hallowe'en a few days later. The lanterns and their bearers representing the spirits of the dead briefly returning from the Land of Shades.

October 31st

Hallowe'en is the most powerful of the three 'spirit nights' of the year. It was a night when the veil between this world and the Other was thin and the dead communicated with the living. Ghosts, demons and witches were abroad and mortals had to protect themselves from the powers of darkness. In Ireland it was said that the faery mounds (prehistoric burial chambers) opened and the Sidhe or Faery Host rode out to roam the countryside. In Wales it was the Ladi Gwyn or White Lady and the Black Sow who chased travellers who were foolish enough to be out and about down lanes.

Hallowe'en, like May Eve and Midsummer Eve, was also a time for divination rites. If a young woman wanted to see who her future lover or husband would be she went out into the garden. On the stroke of midnight she picked a cabbage and it was said the wraith of her future loved one would appear. Alternatively she would later have a dream and see his face. Hemp seed was sown in churchyards and at crossroads (both former pagan sites) by young women at the witching hour on Hallowe'en. After spreading the seed the enquirer called upon her future spouse to appear and collect up the seed. Young lads out for mischief would place a turnip or pumpkin lantern in a tree at the crossroads to scare the women away.

Instead of a cabbage or hemp seed it was said the young women had to pick nine (a lunar number) sage leaves on the ninth stroke of the clock at midnight. If she saw a coffin then she was destined to die an old spinster. Servant girls hung their blouses before the fire at midnight and if one moved as the clock struck its owner would die before the year was out.

The traditional Hallowe'en game of apple-bobbing probably began with divinatory rites to foresee the future. In Wales a large bowl or pan was filled with water and placed in the middle of the floor. Six or eight apples (the number had to be precise) were placed in the bowl so they floated on the water. Single people then took turns to try and bite each apple and remove it from the water. A variant of this was to hang the apples by string from the rafters and the players had to catch the apples in their mouth with their arms tied behind their backs. Whoever was successful was said to be sure of marrying by next Hallowe'en.

Yet another ritual required a young unmarried woman to stand in front of a mirror at midnight while eating an apple and combing her hair. The apparition of her husband-to-be would then materialise in the mirror as if he was looking over her left shoulder. Another version was to cut the apple into nine pieces and throw these over the left shoulder. Then the face of the loved one would appear in the mirror.

Apples were also peeled and the skin was thrown over the shoulder on to the floor, where it was said to form the initials of the would-be husband or lover. Wheat grains and nuts were also thrown on the fire, and if they burned brightly then good luck would last for the coming year. A young man and woman placed cereal grains on a hot shovel and if they all jumped off at the same time in the heat they would marry and have lots of children. Apples were a sacred fruit in Celtic mythology, representing immortality and eternal youth, while grains and nuts were associated with fertility and the harvest just gathered in.

More sinister rites were practised at midnight on the Welsh Border. People went to the church door and listened at the keyhole as an unearthly voice inside recited the names of those who would die in the coming months. It was said that the doors of the pews could be heard opening and shutting and sometimes the wraiths or fetches of those who were to die walked in procession down the church path to the lych gate.

In the 1860's in Laugharne, Carmarthenshire a person was actually appointed to go to the church at midnight on Hallowe'en to hear the names of the dead called out. An old woman in the town was selected and used to stand outside the chancel window listening for the names. Once when she was told that another old lady in the town was dangerously ill and about to die, the listener said she would recover and live for many more years as her name was not among those called on the previous Hallows. This turned out to be true. In another case she foretold that there would soon be a funeral at a certain house and it came to pass.

Today many people, including neo-pagans, believe that 'trick or treat' is a modern American import, yet it was widely practised by our ancestors and probably taken by immigrants to the New World. A prominent feature of so-called 'trick or treating' was the wearing of masks to conceal identity and suggest those involved were demons or spirits of the dead. The Jack O'Lanterns made from turnips, swedes and, more recently, pumpkins had the same purpose. These were hollowed out, cut with a nose, eyes and mouth and a lighted candle was placed inside. They were then put on a pole, stick or wire for carrying. Sometimes these lanterns were hung on gateposts and used as protective guardians to keep spirits away. Today modern children are likely to wear masks and costumes representing Dracula, Spiderman or Freddy from Nightmare on Elm Street, but they are still invoking the same cthonic forces of darkness and the underworld who rule the night of Winter's Eve.

In south Wales men and boys carried out trick or treating wearing women's clothes. They sang a ditty about the White Lady (the Goddess), who sat on top of a tree, pigs (a sacred animal to the Celts and Norse) and apples (a symbol of immortality). In Montgomeryshire these trick or treaters were called gwarchod or Hags and wore sheepskins, ragged clothes and masks in guiser fashion. Sometimes maids exchanged their clothes with male servants for this purpose and at each house apples and nuts were given to the revellers.

When the trick or treaters returned home to the big house or the farm they were rewarded with a traditional supper. This was called 'the mash of nine sorts' and, as the name suggests, it was a stew made from a variety of vegetables including turnips, peas, parsnips, potatoes, carrots and leeks mashed up with pepper, salt and milk. A wedding ring was hidden in it and whoever found it in their bowl was said to be the first to marry. In south Pembrokeshire special cakes, like muffins, were made to be eaten on Hallowe'en and they were washed down with a wassail made of apples, sugar and beer.

In Carmarthenshire the rooms of the farmhouse were decked with evergreens at Hallowe'en, as if it were Christmas. A huge fire was lit in the hearth and apples and nuts were roasted in the flames. These were then added to hot ale, together with raisins, spice and sugar and served in a wassail bowl. Everyone then sat around the fire sipping this drink and telling ghost stories.

Giving out gifts on Hallowe'en

Often in the old days a fire was lit outside 'to keep the witches away'. People gathered around these fires blowing horns to drive away evil spirits and they danced and sang until midnight was passed. Apples and potatoes were roasted in the fire and stones thrown onto it. The next day these stones were removed from the ashes and kept as lucky charms. The main purpose in Scotland for lighting the fires was to combat witchcraft and it was sometimes called 'Burning the Witches'. At Balmoral in Victorian times the effigy of an old woman was thrown on the fire to the sound of bagpipes. It is said that Queen Victoria once attended this folk ritual dating back to the medieval witch hunts, but it is not recorded whether she was amused by it.

In the 1860s the Hallowe'en bonfires were so popular that one traveller through rural Scotland reported seeing thirty blazing on the hillsides and surrounded by rings of dancing figures. This practice continued until before the First World War. Torches were lit at these fires and taken by the servants or children into the fields or around the boundaries of the house or farm. Sometimes it was the parish boundaries that were patrolled in a ritual that seems to have been designed to protect the area from outside evil forces for the year to come.

In the Strathclyde area special Hallowtide cakes or bannocks were made from oatmeal, aniseed, cinnamon and sugar. A space in the house was selected, usually in the kitchen, and marked out as a 'consecrated ground'. Any bystander who wandered into this space while the baking was going on was severely chastised and had to pay a small fine. Six or eight women were chosen as bakers and they sat in a ring to make the dough. The woman who toasted the cakes on a griddle was known as 'The Queen' or 'The Bride'. The dough always had to be passed deosil or sunways around the circle and the first cake was given to a local cuckold, in the hope that the other men in the district would be spared his fate.

McNeill (1938) regards the Hallowe'en bannock as a relic of a pre-Christian rite. He notes that at Samhain the Callieach or Old Queen takes over from the Bride, or Brigid. The marking out of consecrated ground which is forbidden to outsiders, the circle of women, the passing of the dough sunways and the giving of the first cake to a man who has been sexually betrayed are all obvious signs that this folk custom dates back to pagan rites associated with Goddess worship.

November 2nd

Cakes also feature in the custom of 'souling' that took place on this date. Soul cakes were made for distribution around the district or given out to soulers or soul singers who visited each house. The soul cakes were small spiced buns or fruitcakes and in Yorkshire the custom was known as the Soul Mass Cake, in Carmarthenshire as Dole Bread or Soul meat and in North Wales as 'the food of the messenger of the dead'.

When the poor were handed soul cakes they were asked to pray for those who had died during the year and also to God to bless the fields and provide a good harvest in the coming year. When the Roman Church took over the festival they distributed alms to the poor who in return were asked to pray for the souls of the dead. In parts of Wales only those who had helped bring the harvest in were given the cakes.

In Cheshire the soulers were accompanied on their rounds by a hooden horse, a man carrying a horse's skull on a pole and hidden under a white cloth. The skull was painted black and decked with ribbons and bells, with a snappy jaw. He had several nicknames including Old Hob, Old Dick and the Wild Horse. He is associated with a mumming play given on All Soul's Day and featuring St George and the Doctor.

November 4th

Guy Fawkes Eve was known as Mischief Night in the north of England and is yet another example of the topsy-turvy rites marking the beginning of the winter. Young people roamed the streets putting fireworks through letterboxes, whitewashing windows, smearing doorknobs with treacle, filling locks with glue, upturning dustbins and stealing gates for the Bonfire Night next day.

Until the end of the 19th century, Mischief Night coincided with Hallowe'en. We can therefore see that the pranks and tricks played on that night were associated with the activities of fairies and goblins. May Eve was also often called Mischief Night, and that was another time when the faery folk were believed to be out and about pestering and frightening human beings.

November 5th

Since the 17th century this date has marked the anniversary of the Gunpowder Plot in 1605. To begin with the day was only marked by bell ringing and services of thanksgiving for the safety of the king and the members of

Parliament. Gradually it seems the older traditions of the Hallowe'en bonfires were transferred to this date and it became Bonfire Night. Today it is the principal fire festival of the year and merges with Hallowe'en. It is a time for making satirical or anarchic statements and in recent years the effigy of Guy Fawkes has been replaced by current hate figures such as the Pope, Kaiser Wilhelm, Hitler and in the 1980s political figures like Maggie Thatcher and her chancellor, Norman Lamont.

Until the last half of the 19th century blazing tar barrels were a feature of Bonfire Night. At Burford in Oxfordshire these were rolled down the high street, while at nearby Whitley teams competed to push flaming barrels up and down the street. This custom seems to have been very active in the West Country, especially Devon, on Guy Fawkes.

November 11th, Old Hallowe'en, and Martinmas in the Church's calendar, was the feast day of the pagan-hating St Martin of Tours who introduced the monastery into early medieval Europe. It is recorded that he organised and led mobs who toured the countryside burning down druidic groves and murdering their priests.

In Laugharne the dole bread or soul cakes were made on this date and distributed, with sacks of barley and cheese, to the poor people on Old Souls Day. Farmers in Scotland believed that an animal should be killed on this day as it was essential blood was spilt. On the Hebrides no work was done on this day and even women were forbidden to spin or weave.

After the First World War November 11th was selected as Armistice Day, the anniversary of the end of the war. Today this is now observed on the nearest Sunday to the date as Remembrance Day, with the dead honoured by church services at cenotaphs. This day's long association with the dead and the spirit world continues even in these modern times.

The Leaf Man

Chapter Seven

European Folk Festivals

It is almost impossible nowadays to examine the British Isles without including it as part of Europe. Since the last war the political and economic links between Britain and the rest of Europe have been strengthening and this resulted in the foundation of the European Union in 1994, replacing the old EEC. For the last thousand years our principal enemies have been the European powers of France, Germany and Russia, but our links go back further than that.

The 'British' are a mongrel race, or to put it more politely, a cosmopolitan mix of ethnic identities; Iberian, Celts, Romans, German, Norse, Norman-French and Dutch. Our royal family since the ill-fated Stuarts have been Dutch and German and are related to all the crowned heads of Europe. Both the Kaiser and Czar Nicholas were cousins of King George V, so the First World War can be seen as a power struggle between members of the same family.

It is interesting therefore to relate the folk calendar and customs of the British Isles, which includes northern and southern Ireland, with the folk rites and festivals of the Wheel of the Year celebrated across the European continent: and that is the subject of this final chapter.

December 6th

As we have already seen, St Nick's Day was and is a major date in those European countries that were Catholic. In Germany the saint brings his gifts to the children on St Nicholas' Eve, accompanied by his dwarfish manservant Knecht Ruprecht or Hans Muff. Old Nick himself carries a huge book in which all the good and bad deeds of the children are recorded. His servant also carries the bag of goodies for the well behaved children, and a stick to beat those who have been naughty during the year. Originally this was the god or spirit of the winter who has been transformed into a bogey to scare bad children into mending their ways.

Entrance of St Lucia - Goddess of Light

The saint is also sometimes accompanied by a hobby horse known as the Schimnel. This is a white horse represented by a young man hiding under a white cloth. He appears sometimes with a small boy playing the Christchild and several fairy godmothers, old women played by men in dresses with black faces. Their role is to enter the house before the Christchild and chase the children. When the horse arrives he selects one of the young women of the house and chases her until she agrees to dance with him.

December 13th

This is St Lucia's Day and she was said to have been a Sicilian girl of the 4th century who was persecuted for her beliefs and sentenced to be burnt to death. Miraculously when the pyre was lit the flames did not harm her and she had to be stabbed with a sword. Because of this Lucia or Lucy, whose name means 'light', became associated with fires lit to ward off the powers of darkness. In reality these fires were originally lit in pagan times to encourage the sun to be reborn and rise in the sky after the winter solstice.

In the Scandinavian countries Lucy Day, sometimes called Little Yule, was regarded as the beginning of the festive season. Bonfires are lit and a young girl is chosen to be the Lucy Bride or Queen. The chosen one is dressed in a white dress and crowned with a wreath of twigs holding nine burning candles. At sunset this representative of the saint tours the locality visiting houses and farms, where she blesses the livestock. She is accompanied by small children wearing grotesque masks to represent the trolls and spirits of the winter.

In Lucia's native Sicily images of her are paraded through the streets, while in Austria it is believed that witches fly through the night sky on St Lucy's Eve. In other parts of Europe young women perform divination rites praying to the saint to let them see a vision of their future husbands or lovers. All this suggests that this saint took over the role of the northern European sun goddess. In Rome this day was sacred to the corn goddesses Ceres and Demeter, who brought fertility to the land.

St Lucy Day's Queen - bringing gifts to the sick
and elderly

Yule & The Twelve Days the winter solstice on St Thomas' Eve (December 21st) was the day when a special cake called the Keltebrot was cooked. This was made from dried pears, raisins, figs and nuts. Half way through the cooking it was traditional for the cook to go out into the apple orchard and embrace each tree to ensure a good harvest. This is no doubt a watered down version of erotic rites formerly carried out in the orchard for the same purpose.

The solstice was the longest night of the year and was called Spinning Night, because young women would spin through the night to earn extra money for Christmas. In pagan Northern Europe it was known as the Night of the Mothers and it was dedicated to the Norns, the triad of goddesses who weaved the web of wyrd or destiny, and to Holda, the goddess of winter and female leader of the Wild Hunt.

On the longest night, as in Britain, the people stayed up until dawn eating, drinking and playing games. Young women went to bed and slept with their feet on the pillow so they could dream of their future bridegroom. This reversal of the usual sleeping position is typical of the type of behaviour to be found in 'the 'time between time', the Twelve Days between Yule and the New Year.

In Lithuania December 25th was celebrated as the rebirth of the sun who was known in feminine form as Mother Sun. Images of the solar disc were processed through the streets to grant everyone prosperity. People wore animal costumes representing bulls, goats, horses, bears and cranes and a Yule Log was dragged into the house by carol singers. This was burnt in the evening to symbolise the death of the Old Year and afterwards a traditional supper of pork, fruit cake and ashberry wine was consumed.

Swedish Yule Goat - circa 1913

The period between Yule and Twelfth Night across Europe was a time for guising. People sang carols, danced and wore animal masks and costumes. In Scandinavia and Finland the Yule Goats visited houses, bringing good luck and in return were given cakes to eat. If the food is not supplied then the Yule Goats leave in disgust taking the spirit of Christmas with them. Sometimes the Goats also appeared at weddings, emphasising their role as fertility symbols. One was dressed as a woman with horns carrying a sack and a club, while the other is a small boy with goat's ears and horns and wearing 18th century dress.

In Sweden dressing up as Yule Goats was banned in 1695 and anyone who broke this law could face the death penalty. The 'goat' in this case was either a man in a sheepskin and head or a carved goat's head on a stick. In Iceland the ritual disguise was horse or stag and its retinue included the 'shield maidens' - men in women's clothing who sang obscene songs and danced with the animal. Sometimes the stag carried lighted candles in its antlers or another version had a wooden mask with glass eyes and rams' horns, and a body made from sheepskin.

People in the Tyrol also dressed as demons 'to scare winter away'. A troupe of guisers known as the Perchtenmasken (Percht being another name for the winter goddess) danced in the fields to make them fertile. They were led by a man on a white horse and they danced until 'the Old Woman', a witch with a besom, appeared and chased them away.

New Year's Eve

In Eastern Europe guisers were also active around the New Year dressed as bulls, bears and rams. Even under communist rule in the 1950s the New Year Bull rampaged through the villages of southern Poland. This 'bull' was in fact a man dressed in a goat mask, with horns and a snapping jaw, and covered in a ram's fleece. Sometimes he had shoes resembling cloven hooves and brandished a bundle of birch twigs, used as a scourge to punish naughty children and chastise wanton women. Often the New Year Bull was attended by dancers wearing reindeer antlers.

A Yule Goat (left of picture) visits a house at Christmas

In Germany there was an old tradition that the church or town clock chimed thirteen at midnight on New Year's Eve. Village night watchmen climbed to the top of the church tower and welcomed in the New Year by blowing horns. Villagers left their front door open, to let the New Year in, and a back window unlatched so the Old Year could leave. The lads in the village made a straw image of a woman and threw it in the river at midnight before electing the most attractive young woman to be the New Year Queen.

Spring & Easter

In Sardinia the festivities to welcome the spring begin early in the New Year. On January 7th, St Anthony's Day, villagers in mountain areas set three hollow tree trunks ablaze in the square. They then circle them twelve times, once for each month of the year, and smear the ashes of the fire on their faces, to mark the mourning of Demeter for her daughter Persephone, kidnapped by Pluto, Lord of Hades.

A month later a group of twelve guisers, clad in shaggy sheepskins, wearing wooden masks and carrying goat bells, process through the streets in jerky movements like automatons. Folklorists believe that in ancient times these guisers would have been villagers selected as sacrificial victims to encourage the return of spring. In some villages these divine victims are represented by puppets who are burnt on a bonfire by the children. They then smear their faces with ash, don white robes and go out into the night with lanterns 'looking for the spirits of the sacrificed ones'.

On St George's Day (April 23rd) in Mons, Belgium a mumming play was performed with the saint killing the dragon, or summer/light replacing winter/darkness. The two main characters are joined by a procession of fools, Wild Men, covered in green leaves and moss, and hobby horses. The event culminates at midday, when the sun is at its highest in the sky, when George slays the dragon by rather unsportingly shooting it with a pistol. The play is now usually performed on Trinity Sunday in late May.

In the Austrian Alps the chasing away of winter takes place near Shrove Tuesday, when there is still often snow on the high ground. The leader of the guisers is dressed all in red and is known as the Whiffler. It is his task to whiffle, or blow away the winter, while clearing the way for spring with a besom. He leads a group of runners wearing pointed fools' caps and bells who travel with him from farm to farm. At each place they perform a spiralling wheel dance, moving clockwise and anti-clockwise in and out of the house. Sometimes the dancers wear animal masks and there is an Old Woman (winter) carrying a baby (spring).

Spring is celebrated in Lithuania with a ceremony where people whip each other for luck. The earth is also scoured to wake life up and make the plants begin to grow. A special scourge is used for this purpose made from juniper, birch and willow twigs. It is tied together with ribbons and interwoven with flowers and strips of coloured paper.

At Easter coloured eggs are exchanged to symbolise the Cosmic Egg that gave birth to creation. In Germany small Easter eggs are hung on a tree made of green birch twigs placed in a vase. Children walked three times around these 'trees' and then presented them to a young woman, known as the Easter Virgin, who gave them cakes in return. In the Alps these Easter Trees were placed near wells where everyone gathered on Easter Day Eve at midnight to drink the water and sing hymns.

The day before Good Friday was called in German Grundoannerstrag or Green Thursday. On that day it was considered lucky to wear green, eat green foods, take a bath, clean your clothes and clear out your house as spring had arrived officially. Blazing wagon wheels were also rolled down hills in Germany at Easter. The resulting ash was spread on gardens or in the fields to bring good crops.

May Day

Walpurgisnacht or May Eve (April 30th) was widely regarded throughout Europe as the night when the Grand Meeting of all the covens took place. For this reason few people ventured out on that night. If they did it was to attend the witches sabbath or practice protective rituals of counter-magic to protect themselves or their animals from spells.

German women, like their British cousins, got up early on May Day to wash in the morning dew to get rid of blemishes, freckles and warts. Tthe young men made garlands out of birch twigs, tinsel and flowers and hung them outside the windows of women they fancied. In some villages boys used to roam the woods at dawn 'bringing in the summer'. This would be another boy who was hidden. When he was found they decked him with leaves and returned him to the village to marry the May Queen.

Whitsun

This Christian festival was acknowledged in Europe with folk rites dating back to pagan times. They included the crowning, and ritual 'beheading' of the Whitsun King, who was a Jack-in-the-Green type character. In northern France a hobby horse belonging to a secret fraternity of churchwardens makes an appearance at Whitsun. He is escorted by nine men clad in white tabards embroidered with the ancient Goddess symbol, the fleur-de-lys, and two 'policemen' carrying flower decorated druidic wands.

After early morning Mass on Whit Sunday this group go into the woods to chop down a small oak tree. This oak tree is planted in the church grounds and the hobby horse circles it three times. After Vespers the horse circles it another nine times and the assembly read out a long poem describing all the scandals and gossip of the last year in the village.

Midsummer

In Northern Europe midsummer featured the traditional bonfires on St John's Eve and by the raising of Maypoles. In Germany pagan and Christian beliefs were combined in a ceremony where a Maypole and one of its dancers are thrown into a river. They are then hauled out and he is baptised as St John. People also lit midsummer fires and jumped over them to bring good fortune. Young single women were told to be careful, because if they jumped the fire they would become pregnant. While the midsummer fires blazed all others had to be extinguished, and even the blacksmith let his forge go cold.

In Lithuania the Midsummer 'Maypole' was a three pronged branch symbolising the sun, moon and stars. It was crowned with wreaths of wild flowers and coloured ribbons and other wreaths of oak (male) and wild flowers (female) were floated down rivers with candles in them. If

Leaping over the St John's Day bonfire - Alsace 1830

a male and female wreath floated together it was said the couple would become lovers or marry.

People also jumped over the midsummer fires and burnt straw images on them that represented everything old and unwanted. If a married couple held hands to jump the fire and lost their grip it was said they would soon divorce. Newlyweds collected the ashes to take home as symbols of harmony and fertility. After the dawn was greeted a special breakfast was eaten in the fields like a picnic, with cheese, eggs and beer laid out on a white or gold cloth sprinkled with cut herbs.

Harvest End

The ceremony of cutting the last sheaf was widely practised across Europe and Frazer gives many examples. In 19th century Russia the female farm worker who cut the last sheaf was called the Old Man, in a neat example of gender reversal. The last sheaf was called by the same name and at the Harvest Supper the farm worker could pick any man to be her dancing partner, sat at the top of the table and was given the best food. If the sheaf gatherer was a man he had to wear women's clothes and a black mask covering all his face.

In Germany passing strangers were seized by the farm workers and wrapped up in the last sheaf. They could only escape by paying a small ransom or promising to buy everyone a drink at the inn. In other cases it was the farmer who was lured to the field by a false message and then forced to become a human last sheaf. Such strange customs obviously have echoes of ritual sacrifice when an unsuspecting stranger became the substitute Corn King. As in Britain, alternative names for the last sheaf were the Old Woman, the Maiden and the Bride.

The ritual gathering of the last sheaf was symbolic of the capture of the spirit of the corn, who was held captive in the barn or house during the winter until his/her life-giving energy was needed to fertilise the land in the spring. The sacrifice of the divine king allowed his blood to fertilise the fields during the dark season, when the God is in the underworld. Fertility rites in the spring, which in the

European context included naked women pulling the plough around a field, revitalised his blood so his life energy ensured a good harvest at summer's end.

Folk memories of such bloody and primitive rites can be found in the flax growing areas of Austria. There the women who gather in the harvest are formed into guilds and are visited at the end of the flax gathering by a White Horse and a sooty faced 'smith' and his 'wife', who is played by a young boy. The Horse kills the wife by trampling on her and then the Knacker arrives, complete with large

Traditional Scandanavian Corn Dolly

artificial phallus, and proceeds to revive her from the dead by sexual congress.

During the flax gathering no men are allowed in the drying room. If one dares to enter he is dragged to the ground, roughly kissed and has his face blackened. A Corn Maiden is made of flax and sprinkled with holy water from the church. At the end of harvest the women dance with this image, but if any man dares to witness this he is dragged to the ground, beaten and wildly kissed by all the women.

Winter's Night

Around the end of October and the beginning of November farmers all over Europe bring their livestock down from the summer pastures. In the Alps the farmer and his wife put on their Sunday best clothes for this task. The cows are dressed up as well, with ribbons, flowers and feathers on their horns and heavy leather collars hung with bells. The farmer and his wife set off at dawn to bring in the cows and they have to be back before dusk settles.

Lithuanians celebrated their own festival for the dead after Harvest Home. It went on throughout October and ended on the first weekend in November. When Christianity came it was confined to All Soul's Day (November 2nd), but was still called by its pagan name of the Festival of Veles i.e. the shades of the dead. It was a time for remembering and honouring dead relatives and ancestors. A special meal was eaten with an extra place laid for the dead, and the doors and windows were left open so they come and go. After the meal the graves of the family were visited, candles were lit, libations of red wine poured over the earth and scraps of food from the meal left as offerings.

On our grand tour of European folk traditions, rituals and festivals the similarities between them and their British counterparts, allowing for cultural differences, have been remarkable. All over Europe the agricultural year, the changing seasons and the solar festivals were celebrated with folk rituals, superstitions and symbols that pre-date Christianity. As we have seen, in many cases Christian and pagan beliefs have become hopelessly entangled. This is common not only to Europe, but also to Africa, the Caribbean and South America, where the new religion grafted itself on the indigenous spirituality to create a hybrid belief-system.

That these ancient religious rituals honouring Nature and the land have survived at all in the face of Christian persecution and intolerance, and the march of materialistic progress is a miracle in itself. Today many thousands of people are seeking to re-connect with their natural roots in the face of an out-of-control consumer society that seems destined to pollute and destroy the environment of our planet. This 'green revolution' is supported by the modern revival of the Old Ways. Many members of the new pagan movement are sincerely seeking inspiration from the folk traditions of their ancestors.

In the European world of real-politick, with the obscenity of butter mountains rotting in warehouses while the Third World starves, the need for the type of fertility rites described in this book may seem redundant. However it is also unfortunate that modern factory farming methods are degrading and destroying our countryside. Hedges rich in fauna and flora are being ripped out to create large fields open to soil erosion, while each years millions of pounds are spent on chemical fertilisers with unknown side-effects for coming generations.

While nobody is suggesting that these fertilisers are replaced by human blood, it is tempting to think that farmers could cultivate a more harmonious relationship with the spirit of the land, rather then raping Mother Earth for short-term benefits. When I look out of my cottage window and watch the farmer next door driving across his land on a three-wheeled motorbike to round up sheep, his Sony Walkman clamped over his ears, I sometimes wonder how close to Nature the average country person is nowadays.

At the close of the first chapter I emphasised how important the Wheel of the Year is to our spiritual, and physical, wellbeing. Today we tend to mark the passing of the year by socio-cultural events or over-commercialised 'Christian' festivals like Christmas and Easter, the New Year, exams or summer holidays. All these can be experienced and enjoyed in their own right, but we also need to find time in our hyperactive existence to sit back and acknowledge an older pattern of events based on the sun, the moon, the stars and the changing seasons that make up the Sacred Ring of the Wheel of the Year.

A British Folk Calendar

January

1st	New Year
6th	Twelfth Night
	Haxey Hood Game
	Plough Monday
17th	Wassailing the apple orchards

February

1st	Imbolc
2nd	Candlemass
14th	St Valentine's Day
	Shrove Tuesday
	Pancake Day

March

21st/22nd	Vernal Equinox
	Eostre/Easter

April

1st	All Fool's Day
23rd	St George's Day
30th	May Eve/Walpurgis Night

May

1st	May Day or Beltane
8th	Furry Dance
13th	Garland Day
Last Monday	Whitsun/Spring Holiday
	Ram Fair
29th	Oak Apple Day

June

21st/22nd	Summer Solstice
23rd	Midsummer Eve
24th	Midsummer Day

August

1st	Lughnasadh
2nd	Lammas
10th	Well Dressing
11th/12th	Burryman Parade
	Puck Fair
24th	Burning the Bartle

September

4th	Abbots Bromley Horn Dance
21st/22nd	Autumn Equinox
29th	Michaelmas

October

Last Thursday	Punkie Night
31st	Hallowe'en

November

1st	All Saints Day/Samhain
2nd	All Souls' Day
4th	Mischief Night
5th	Bonfire Night
11th	Martinmas

December

6th	St Nicholas' Day
21st/22nd	Winter Solstice/Yule
24th	Christmas Eve
25th	Christmas Day
26th	Boxing Day
31st	New Year's Eve

... and so the Wheel of the Year turns again.

Contacts

For further information on the pagan Old Religion, folklore and seasonal customs contact the following. Enclose a stamped addressed envelope with all enquiries.

The Cauldron
Caemorgan Cottage
Caemorgan Road
Cardigan
Dyfed
SA43 1QU

Tradition
P. O. Box 57
Hornchurch
Essex
RM11 1DU

The Folklore Society,
c/o University College, London,
Gower Street
London WC1E 6BT

Bibliography

Alford, V. The Hobby Horse & Other Animal Masks (the Merlin Press 1978)

Anderson, W & Hicks, C   The Green Man (Harper Collins 1990)

Baker, M   Discovering Christmas Customs & Folklore (Shire Publications 1968)

Folklore & Customs of Rural England (David & Charles 1974)

Batsford, K.M. The Green Man (D.S. Brewer 1978)

Cawte, F. Ritual Animal Disguise (D.S.Brewer 1978)

Earp, F.   May Day in Nottinghamshire (Heart of Albion Press 1991)

Evans, C.   The Horse in the Furrow (Faber 1960)
            The Pattern Under the Plough (Faber 1966)
            The Farm & the Village (Faber 1969)

Farrar, J. & S.   Eight Sabbats for Witches (Robert Hale 1981)

Frazer, J.   The Golden Bough (Oxford University Press 1922)

Helm, A.   The English Mummer's Play (D.S.Brewer 1981)

Hole, C.   British Folk Customs (Hutchinson 1976)

Jones, N.   Power of Raven, Wisdom of Serpent (Floris 1994)

Judge, R .   Jack-in-the-Creen (D.S. Brewer 1979)

Leather, E.M.   The Folklore of Herefordshire (Jakeman & Carver 1912)

Muir, F & J   A Treasury of Christmas (Robson Books 1981)

Murray, Dr M.   The God of the Witches (OUP 1931)

McCrickard, J.   Brighde (Feildfare Arts & Design 1987)

Mc Neill, F.M.   The Silver Bough Vols I-IV (MacLellan 1959)

Newall, V.   An Egg at Easter (Routledge 1971)

Owen, T.   Welsh Folk Customs (Welsh Folk Museum 1959)

Palmer C & Lloyd, N.   A Year of Festivals (Frederick Warne 1972)

Pegg, B   Rites & Riots (Blandford Press 1991)

Shipman, F.   The Abbots Bromley Horn Dance (The Benhill Press 1982)

Simpson, J.   The Folklore of the Welsh Border (Batsford 1976)

Stewart, R   Where is St George? (Moonraker Press 1977)

Straffon, C   Pagan Cornwall (Meym Mamvro 1993)

Taylor, I The Giant of Penhill (Northern Lights 1987)

Thoinger, R   A Calendar of German Customs (Oswald Wulff 1966)

Trubshaw, R   Dragon Slaying Myths (Heart of Albion Press 1993)

Valiente, D   Where Witchcraft Lives (Aquarian Press 1962)

Williamson, J   The Oak King, the Holly King & the Unicorn (Harper Row 1986)

Index

Other Titles Published by Capall Bann

A selection of other titles published by Capall Bann. A detailed illustrated catalogue is available on request, SAE or International Postal Coupon appreciated. Titles are available from good bookshops and specialist outlets, or direct from Capall Bann, post free in the UK (send cheque or postal order).

Animals, Mind Body Spirit & Folklore
Angels and Goddesses - Celtic Christianity & Paganism by Michael Howard
Animal Magics by Gordon 'The Toad' Maclellan
Arthur - The Legend Unveiled by C Johnson & E Lung
Auguries and Omens - The Magical Lore of Birds by Yvonne Aburrow
Book of the Veil The by Peter Paddon
Call of the Horned Piper by Nigel Jackson
Cats' Company by Ann Walker
Celtic Lore & Druidic Ritual by Rhiannon Ryall
Compleat Vampyre - The Vampyre Shaman: Werewolves & Witchery by Nigel Jackson
Crystal Clear - A Guide to Quartz Crystal by Jennifer Dent
Earth Dance - A Year of Pagan Rituals by Jan Brodie

Earth Magic by Margaret McArthur
Enchanted Forest - The Magical Lore of Trees by Yvonne Aburrow
Healing Home by Jennifer Dent
In Search of Herne the Hunter by Eric Fitch
Inner Space Workbook - Developing Counselling & Magical Skills Through the Tarot
Living Tarot by Ann Walker
Magical Lore of Animals by Yvonne Aburrow
Magical Lore of Cats by Marion Davies

Magical Lore of Herbs by Marion Davies
Masks of Misrule - The Horned God & His Cult in Europe by Nigel Jackson
Mysteries of the Runes by Michael Howard
Oracle of Geomancy by Nigel Pennick
Patchwork of Magic by Julia Day
Pathworking - A Practical Book of Guided Meditations by Pete Jennings
Pickingill Papers - The Origins of Gardnerian Wicca by Michael Howard
Psychic Animals by Dennis Bardens
Psychic Self Defence - Real Solutions by Jan Brodie

Sacred Grove - The Mysteries of the Forest by Yvonne Aburrow
Sacred Geometry by Nigel Pennick
Sacred Lore of Horses The by Marion Davies
Sacred Ring - Pagan Origins British Folk Festivals & Customs by Michael Howard
Secret Places of the Goddess by Philip Heselton
Taming the Wolf - Full Moon Meditations by Steve Hounslow
West Country Wicca by Rhiannon Ryall
Wildwood King by Philip Kane
Witches of Oz The by Matthew & Julia Phillips

Womens Studies
Menopausal Woman on the Run by Jaki da Costa

Environmental Education
Talking to the Earth by Gordon Maclellan

Capall Bann is owned and run by people actively involved in many of the areas in which we publish. Our list is expanding rapidly so do contact us for details on the latest releases. We guarantee our mailing list will never be released to other companies or organisations.

Capall Bann Publishing, Freshfields, Chieveley, Berks, RG16 8TF.

Latest Titles From Capall Bann. Full catalogue available on request.

Cat's Company - A book of cats and - history - reincarnation - healing - communication - stories
By Ann Walker

Ann explores the role of the cat through history, from being worshipped in Ancient Egypt to being cruelly treated and hated in Medieval Europe. The book includes tales of cats who returned to their owners after death, both in spirit and reincarnated form. Stating that "The Ancient Celts believed that the eyes of a cat were windows through which humans could explore the inner world", we are given an extract from a grimoire giving guidance on how to attune yourself to your cat. Believing in the healing power of cats and our ability to think/talk with them, Ann shares many stories of the cats she has known and loved over the years. A fascinating and enthralling book for cat lovers everywhere.

ISBN 1 898307 32 6   Price £10.95

Psychic Animals - A fascinating investigation of paranormal behaviour
By Dennis Bardens Foreword by David Bellamy

".......remarkably interesting & totally 'different' book on the mysterious powers displayed by animals of all kinds........those who read it will find themselves observing animals, & perhaps themselves too, in an entirely new light." David Bellamy

For centuries animals of all kinds have displayed amazing powers of psychic intelligence as bizarre & inexplicable as the strangest human paranormal experiences. Fascinating accounts of unusual animal behaviour include the stories of the horse that helped police locate the body of a murdered baby, the stowaway dog that sailed 5,000 miles to find his master & the seagull that sought help for an injured woman. In this unique study, internationally known psychic investigator Dennis Bardens presents a persuasive body of evidence revealing & explaining remarkable feats of animal telepathy, precognition & long-distance perception.

ISBN 1 898307 39 3   Price £10.95   210 pages   Illustrated

Psychic Self Defence - Real Solutions By Jan Brodie

How to recognise a psychic attack & how to handle it? This book concentrates on a commonsense approach to problems including interviews describing how people have dealt with attacks. Practical information, based on real experiences, is given on a range of protective & self development measures:- Summoning a guardian. Coping with psychic attack during magical or circle work, Banishing 'evil' influences, Holding your own in the Otherworlds/Astral levels. Protective amulets & talismans, Strengthening the aura, Avoiding the pitfalls on the occult path, Increasing self-confidence in magical work & visualisation, Psychic attack - What it is & What it is not, Elemental Spirits of Nature, Guardian Spirits, the Aura, the Astral Levels, the Psychic Vampire, the Realm of Faerie, Ghosts, Psychic Attack Through Willpower & the Evil Eye.

Price £8.95   ISBN 1 898307 36 9   190 pages   Illustrated

Sacred Geometry - Symbolism and Purpose in Religious Structures
by Nigel Pennick

Geometry underlies the structure of all things - from galaxies to molecules. Despite our separation from the natural world, we human beings are still bounded by the laws of the universe. Each time a geometrical form is created, an expression of this universal oneness is made & from the dawn of time religious structures have expressed this unity in their every detail. In this absorbing history, the first of its kind, the applications of sacred geometry are examined & the full extent of its practise is revealed. Sacred geometry is responsible for the feeling of awe generated by a gothic cathedral & the 'rightness' of a Georgian drawing-room. Sacred Geometry traces the rise & fall of this transcendent art from megalithic stone circles to Art Nouveau & reveals how buildings that conform to its timeless principles mirror the geometry of the cosmos.

ISBN 1 898307 156   Price £9.95   190 pages   Illustrated

In Search of Herne the Hunter   By Eric Fitch

Commences with an introduction to Herne's story, going on to investigates antlers & their symbology in prehistoric religions, with a study of the horned god Cernunnos, the Wild Hunt & its associations with Woden, Herne & the Christian devil & a descriptive chapter on the tradition of dressing up as animals & the wearing & use of antlers in particular. Herne's suicide & its connection with Woden & prehistoric sacrifice is covered, together with the most complete collection of Herne's appearances, plus an investigation into the nature of his hauntings. The final section brings all the strands together, with additional material. Photographs, illustrations & diagrams enhance the authoritative & well researched text. The book also contains appendices covering the 19th century opera on the legend of Herne, Herne & his status in certain esoteric circles & Herne & Paganism/Wicca.

ISBN 1 898307 237   Price £9.95   167 pages   35 b/w illustrations & photos

Crystal Clear - A Guide to Quartz Crystal By Jennifer Dent

This book answers the need for a basic and concise guide to quartz crystal - solving the many confusions and contradictions that exist about this fascinating topic, without being too esoteric or straying too far from the point. Crystals particularly clear quartz crystals, evoke a response, which can not be rationally explained; they inspire a sense of the sacred, of mystery, magic and light. This book explores why crystals are important, their place in history, cleansing, clearing, charging, energising/programming your crystals and techniques for using them for healing. Also included is a chapter on the formation & scientific aspects of quartz which is written in a humourous style to help offset the generally mind-numbing effects of talking physics with non-physicists. Jennifer has worked with crystals for many years, using them for healing & other purposes.

ISBN 1 898307 30 X   Price £7.95   120 pages   Illustrated

The Call of the Horned Piper   by Nigel Aldcroft Jackson

Covers the symbolism, archetypes & myths of the Traditional Craft, or Old Religion, in the British Isles & Europe. Starting with an exploration of the inner symbology & mytho-poetics of the old Witchcraft religion, this is followed by a practical treatment of the sacred cycle, the working tools, incantations, spells & pathworking. There are also sections on spirit lines, knots & thread lore & magic, together with ancestral faery teachings. The text is highlighted with the author's superb original artwork. A radical & fresh re-appraisal of authentic witch-lore which may provide a working alternative to current mainstream trends in Wicca.

"A practical grimoire of the ancient & traditional ways of witchcraft... .the most important book on witchcraft since Gerald Gardner's 'Witchcraft Today'. Highly recommended'
The Cauldron

ISBN 1 898307 091   Price £8.95   117 pages   29 b/w illustrations

Angels & Goddesses - Celtic Christianity & Paganism in Ancient Britain by Michael Howard

Traces the history & development of Celtic Paganism & Celtic Christianity specifically in Wales, but also in relation to the rest of the British Isles including Ireland, from the Iron Age to the present day. There follows a study of the transition between the old pagan religions & Christianity & how the early Church, especially in the Celtic countries, both struggled with & later absorbed the earlier forms of spirituality it encountered. This can be clearly seen in the history of early Christianity in Roman Britain & in the later development of Celtic Christianity when pagan & Christian beliefs co-existed, albeit in an uneasy & sometimes violent relationship.

How the Roman Catholic version of Christianity arrived in England at the end of the 6th century & its affect on the Celtic Church; how Celtic Christianity was suppressed & the effect this was to have on the history & theology of the Church in the Middle Ages. The influence of Celtic Christianity on the Arthurian legends & the Grail romances is explored. Finally the resurgence of interest in Celtic Christianity today is covered & how, despite attempts to eradicate it from the pages of clerical history, its ideas & ideals have survived, are influencing New Age concepts & are relevant to the critical debate about the future of the modern church.

ISBN 1 898307 032   Price £9.95   169 pages

The Mysteries of the Runes By Michael Howard

Not just another book of how to cast the runes, but a full investigation into their origins, symbolism & use. Their origin is traced from Neolithic & Bronze Age symbols & their connection with other magical & mystical symbols. Runic divination by Germanic tribes & the Saxons together with the Viking use of runes are also covered. The Norse god Odin is discussed, as the shaman-god of the runes, with his myths & legends, the Wild Hunt, the Valkyries & his connections with the Roman god Mercury, Thoth, Jesus & the Odinic mysteries. Magical uses of runes are explored with their use in divination. Fascinating information is included on discoveries made in archaeological excavations, rune masters & mistresses, the bog sacrifices of Scandanavia & the training of the rune master.

Runic symbolism & their place in pre-Christian society is explored. Detailed descriptions are given with divinity, religious symbolism & spiritual meanings based on The Anglo Saxon Rune Poem. Details on how to make your own set of runes, how to cast them for divination with examples of rune readings with suggested layouts & the use of rune magic. The final section covers Bronze Age Scandanavia & its religious belief systems; the gods & goddesses of the Aesir & Vanir, their myths & legends & the seasonal cycle of festivals in the Northern Tradition.

ISBN   189830 707 5   Price £9.95   206 pages   42 b/w illustrations

The Pickingill Papers - The Origin of the Gardnerian Craft
by W. E. Liddell   Compiled & Edited by Michael Howard

George Pickingill (1816 - 1909) was said to be the leader of the witches in Canewdon, Essex. This book discusses the origin of the Gardnerian Book of Shadows and Pickingill's involvement in it. Also covered are the relationship between the Hereditary Craft, Gardnerian Wicca & Pickingill's Nine Covens, the influence of Freemasonry on the medieval witch cult, sex magic, the use of quartz globes to boost power, ley lines & earth energy, prehistoric shamanism, the East Anglian lodges of cunning men & Celtic wise women. Here, for the first time, is a chance for the complete Pickingill material to be read & examined together with background references & extensive explanatory notes, new material on the Craft Laws, the New Forest coven & Pickingill's influence on the Revived Craft.

ISBN   1 898307 10 5   Price £9.95   177 pages